Windows 7
ABSOLUTE
BEGINNER

Paragon Publishing Ltd
Paragon House
St Peter's Rd
Bournemouth
Dorset BH1 2JS
United Kingdom

Tel: +44 (0)1202 299900
Fax: +44 (0)1202 299955
Email: books@paragon.co.uk
Web: http://www.paragon.co.uk

Windows for the Absolute Beginner
© 1998 Paragon Publishing Ltd

British Library Cataloguing-in-Publication Data
A catalogue for this book is available from the British Library

ISBN 1-873650-60-4

Designed by: Philip Terrett
Compiled by: John Taylor
Printed & Bound in the UK by: Mackays of Chatham, Badger Road, Lordswood, Chatham, Kent, ME5 8TD
Published by: Paragon Publishing Ltd, Bournemouth

Contents

Absolute Beginners

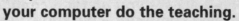

A new computer user can often feel baffled and when it comes down to learning how to use your PC it's sometimes better to let your computer do the teaching.

We deal with the absolute basics, from equipment to the setup of Windows on your PC.

Learn how to use your keyboard and your mouse to make short work of documents.

An extensive Jargon Buster to help you get your head around technical terms.

Find your way round your computer in next to no time

Absolute Beginners: the first hour

Your all-important first hour with Windows should hopefully set you up for a confident future with your new computer – we show you how to get familiar with this novel environment

When you watch experienced computer users starting their machines and getting down to work on one or more tasks the new user can often feel a bit baffled and a little bewildered.

In many ways, it is a bad idea to ask someone else to show you how to use a computer. Often they take over and just do vital preliminary steps for you, leaving you no wiser next time round. In fact, the PC itself is the best teacher when it comes to Windows, which is the name given to its operating environment. There are a number of once-only steps to go through when you switch on your computer for the first time. These days, Windows 98 will almost certainly have been loaded onto the computer for you so there's nothing at all complicated about it. You'll be guided through the procedure by the Setup Wizard. Wizards are something that you'll quickly get acquainted with – essentially they are forms to fill in accompanied by clear instructions and any information required to help you make choices. The very first form asks you for your name, which you simply type on the keyboard. Next comes the Licence Agreement. You are expected to read this and then click the option 'I accept the Agreement.' The third important step is to enter the Product Key found on the Certificate of Authenticity. This will normally be found on the front cover of the 'Getting Started' booklet and is a 25-character code entered as five sets of five letters and numbers. This part is vitally important as no other code will unlock Windows. Once all this information has actually been supplied, then the Windows 98 Setup starts and will take approximately half an hour to complete.

Welcome to Windows 98

The Welcome to Windows 98 screen appears when you first start your PC and is the best starting point for the new user to find out how to work in Windows. Our advice to new users would be to go straight to 'Discover Windows 98'. Included in its Computer Essential section is instruction on how to use the mouse.

This dialog opens automatically with clock chimes and a snatch of music. Its top bar will be bright blue, indicating that it is the active window (in other words, the current or enabled one). As you move the mouse pointer

over the four items in its contents list they 'light up' in turn. When the green background shows, click once on the mouse button. The tick next to 'Connect to the Internet' indicates that this task (which has a step-by-step Wizard to help you) has been completed.

Once you no longer require the Welcome to Windows screen, click this box to remove the tick. To close this screen and get on with the tasks you want to do, click Close. Clicking X is a shortcut to closing the active window and has exactly the same effect as a press of the Close button.

If you are new to the world of Windows then we strongly recommend you take the Microsoft tour, it will show you the absolute basics and essentials

The Initial Desktop

The desktop is the name given to the screen that shows your personalised workspace. The fact that you can customise it means that your desktop may look slightly different to the one here – and as time goes on it will be increasingly different as more items get added to it. You can even change its entire look by choosing a desktop theme. Here's what you should find on a basic desktop:

Icons – Initially the desktop has only a few icons on it for facilities that have been installed at the same time as Windows itself. Clicking on an icon selects it. You can move an icon once selected by dragging with the mouse. Double-clicking opens or activates it. Bot the Internet Explorer and Outlook Express icons are examples of icons that will automatically run programs when clicked on.

My Computer – This useful icon gives easy access to the components of your computer and facilities for managing them. Double-click to open a dialog with icons for the hard drive and floppy disk drive and CD or DVD drive and folders for printers and the Control Panel. You'll use My Computer a lot!

Start Menu – The Start button is at the far left of the taskbar, which is the grey strip at the bottom of the screen. Clicking it once opens the Start Menu, in many ways the heart of Windows, which gives you access to all the options open to you for working with the computer. Where an arrow appears to the right of an item in the menu it means that there are further choices. The Shut Down item in the menu is one to get to know early on and Help is also a menu item worth exploring.

System Tray – The area to the far right of the taskbar acts as a repository for useful tools, hence its name System Tray. By default it contains icons for the Clock, the Volume control and the Task Scheduler. Double-clicking on these icons opens the tools and also lets you adjust them.

Icons on the taskbar – The taskbar has icons that duplicate ones on the desktop or in the Start menu. They give you quick access to commonly required operations from within any application since the taskbar is normally visible when you are working on any task. The desktop icon can be used to switch back to the desktop when you have an application open.

Volume control – Clicking once on the loudspeaker icon in the system tray brings up this volume control that lets you set the overall loudness of the speaker output and mute all sound by ticking a box.

As you install your own programs, some of them may take advantage of the taskbar to offer easy access to features. With the correct tools you will be changing resolution and colour depth, keeping an eye on incoming emails and your online time as well as many other tasks.

So far, you have learnt your way around the very essentials

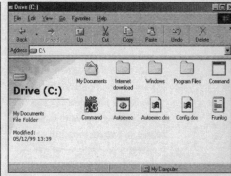

of the desktop, if you are unsure of anything, keep practicing until you know what all the elements do and you are confident of using them. Now we can start exploring beyond the flesh of the basic desktop and into the meat and bones of Windows, the place where most of your work with the PC will take place.

My Computer

From the desktop, double-clicking My Computer will open the My Computer folder in a new window. What you see here will depend on how your PC system has been put together. You will probably see the icon for drive A: showing a diskette above a drive with a slit. Next, you'll probably see

Your C drive is where everything gets saved to when you use any files. Keep things organised by using the Program Files and the My Documents folders

the icon for your hard disk drive, again with a custom name or label followed by (C:). This raises the question 'Why isn't there a B:?' When personal computers were first available, hard disk storage was too expensive to include and so two diskette drives – A: and B: – were the norm. These days, the floppy drive has a relatively minor role and most systems will have the CD with Windows icon indicating a CD or DVD drive. This will often be labelled D: but not necessarily – you can use letters of the alphabet up to M. You will sometimes want to install software from CD-ROMs so it's important to know what letter is used.

There are three controls at the very right of the My Computer window title bar. Going from left to right, these are: Minimise, Maximise and Close the window. When you click on Minimise, the My Computer window closes and you'll find yourself back on the Desktop. Look at the Taskbar. You'll see that a bar called My Computer has appeared there.

You should click on it to re-open the folder.

Click on the Maximise icon to make this window fill the entire screen, that is be a 'full screen' window. Notice how the middle icon has now changed – clicking it restores the window to its former state as a resizable window, and is therefore called the Restore button. Click the Restore button and look for the three diagonal lines at the bottom-right corner of the window. If you put your cursor over this corner it changes to a double-headed arrow. Depress the mouse button and drag in either direction to shrink or expand the window. Click once on the hard disk (C:) icon

There are three controls at the very right of the My Computer (when in a large or full screen window) and compare what you see with this display.

There are two alternative views of any folder. There is Web Page view, for example, and you can recognise it by the name of the folder and its icon against the blue sky

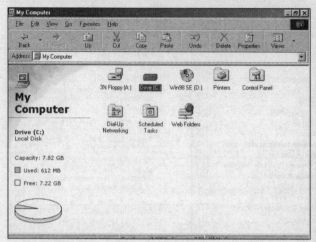

My Computer is where you can access all your storage devices from floppies to CDs and your communications gear including modems

background. If this is not what you see, open the View menu and click on 'as Web Page' to place a tick besides it. The advantage of Web Page view is that it provides information about the currently selected item. With drive C: selected you see an overview of its Capacity and how much of it is free. Clicking the Up button from My Computer goes to the Desktop – but you now view it as a folder displayed in Web Page view.

Here's what else you'll find in the My Computer folder:

The Printers folder, where you can connect a new printer or change the settings for existing ones.

The Control Panel folder, which is used to customise almost every aspect of how your computer works.

Double-clicking on an icon in the My Computer folder opens it. Here we have double-clicked Disk (C:), as the title shown at the top-left indicates.

From here, the Up button goes to My Computer. Look closely, and you should note that the Back button is now active – it goes to the previously open folder, which in this case is also My Computer.

The hard disk has folders on it for both Programs and Data.

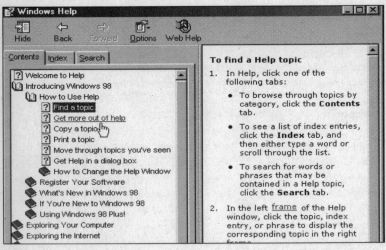

Help is the first place to turn when you don't understand something. Most common problems can be solved here

The folders that you'll find pre-supplied are My Documents, Program Files and Windows. When you have an item selected you see relevant details to the left and size information in the bottom bar.

Windows Help

Clicking Help in the Start Menu opens this comprehensive resource that can answer all your questions about Windows. It is arranged like a book with chapters devoted to topics and sections with chapters covering sub-topics. These are all arranged under three tabbed sections, which are namely:

Content; Index and Search.

The first of these presents the Contents list. If you want details about a specific issue then you need to click the Index tab and look it up in an alphabetical list, or click Search and type in a keyword for the information you want to find. Click the Contents tab to go back to the listing shown here.

Windows Help is displayed in a resizable window with two panes. Having selected a topic you can use the Hide button to close the left panel so that less screen area is devoted to Help – this is useful when you want relevant help on something that's currently happening on the screen.

Click on a closed book icon to open it and display the list of its contents. Click on an open book icon to close it again removing the detailed contents from view. Click on a topic to highlight its name and display it in the viewing pane. As you move the cursor over topics they appear in blue with underlining and can be selected by clicking.

The Getting Started Book – Online Version is a very useful resource. It does more than simply let you read a manual on the screen as it has hyperlinks to jump directly to related information. You should click on text displayed in blue to go directly to these cross-references.

Is this the end? Shut down your machine through the menu rather than the off button if you want to make sure you've saved all your information

Shutting Down

If you only get to know one item in the Start Menu in your first session it has to be Shut Down. This is the only correct way to turn off your machine (although like most other computer operations, it does have a keyboard shortcut that experienced computer users will often use, making everything mysterious again to the novice).

So, in order to turn off your computer the correct way, click Start and then click Shut Down. Select Shut down from the menu that appears. There are occasions when you will be asked to restart your computer. To do this, click Start, click Shut down and then select Restart.

Final Word

It is possible for the taskbar, and with it the Start button, to disappear from view. If this happens, hover the cursor at the extreme bottom-left of the screen (where you expect to see Start in other words) and it will then magically re-appear. Happy computing!

Absolute Beginners:
the mouse

If you are a total PC novice, then this is the best place for you. For the opening guide, we are going to take a look at what you can achieve with just the mouse...

The mouse is an important part of your PC and when it comes to selecting all those icons, buttons and menus there's no doubt it's the best tool for the job.

Mice come in all different shapes and sizes but they all have the same basic elements – a main body that you guide around and two buttons at the end. Some mice have extra bells and whistles, such as scrollwheels and additional buttons, but we'll concentrate on the key parts first.

The Basics

If you haven't used a mouse before it can be a bit of a stumbling block, but learning to use one is easy, so let's get acquainted with it.

The mouse is, quite simply, a pointing device. On your computer screen there is a little arrow, also known as the cursor. As you move the mouse around on your desk, the arrow moves around on the screen. Move the mouse to the left and the arrow moves to the left, move the mouse down and the arrow moves down on the screen. So, using the mouse, you can point the arrow at different things on the screen such as buttons, menus and icons.

To allow you to interact with these items, mice have buttons built into them, and a PC mouse has at least two of these. The left button is used to select things on screen, allowing menus, icons and so on to be either selected/

Wheel
Most recent mice now offer a small central wheel that allows you to scroll through wordprocessor documents, Web pages and other large documents by rolling the wheel up or down. The wheel also acts as a third button

Left button
This is the primary mouse button. If you need to select anything, use this button

Right button
The secondary, or context sensitive menu button, is the right one. While using a program, press this to get a menu of options relevant to the current item under the mouse pointer

Body
You normally rest the palm of your hand on this area to make it as easy as possible to guide the mouse around the tabletop or the mouse mat

chosen/pressed/clicked (the terminology varies). For example, if you move the arrow over the Start button in the bottom left of the screen and press the left mouse button, a new window will pop up. You have just selected the Start button with a single click of the left mouse button.

If you now move the arrow over the My Computer icon at the top left of the screen and press the left button twice in quick succession (known as a double-click), you will open the My Computer window.

Double-clicks are used when you want to open a program, file or drawer. Single-clicks of the left mouse button are used when you want to select something such as a button, file or menu.

The right mouse button opens what is called the context sensitive menu. Almost everything you see on the screen can have certain actions performed on it. If you place the cursor (or arrow) over the My Computer icon and press the right mouse button, a menu appears with the list of actions that can currently be performed. The menu is known as context sensitive because the contents of the menu changes depending on what the mouse cursor is over at the time. This happens in Windows and in

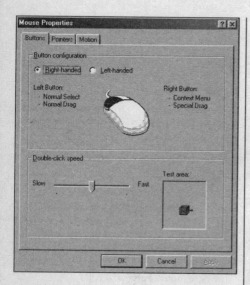

This is the basic Windows mouse control panel, but yours could very well be different

allows you to speed up or slow down the speed of the mouse and the speed of the double-click to a level you are comfortable with.

Control Panel

If you find you are having trouble either double-clicking or even just moving the mouse around Windows it could be well worth taking a look at the mouse control panel from which you can adjust a number of important functions, such as the speed the mouse moves.

Select Start/ Settings/ Control Panel/ Mouse to open the Mouse Properties control panel. This panel may vary a little depending on the exact type of mouse you have, but we'll look at the basic one.

The double-click speed is on the first tab and is something that many people have trouble with. Use the bottom slider to increase the time you have to complete a double-click. The third Motion tab is where you slow down or speed up how quickly the cursor moves around the screen. If you have

most programs that you run under Windows.

What we have covered up to now is enough to get you started with running and using programs. If you find that the mouse moves too quickly or you are having trouble double-clicking, you'll be pleased to discover that the speed of the mouse and double-clicks can be changed. Left-click on the Start button, click on Settings and then Control Panel. This will open a new window. Find the Mouse icon and double-click it. The Mouse Control Panel

extra mouse cursors installed, use the Pointers tab to pick other styles, including larger pointers which are easier to see. If you have a Microsoft wheel mouse, the Basic tab will take care of its functions.

Drag and Drop

The drag and drop function is performed using the mouse. Instead of a single or double-click, you simply place the mouse cursor over a file's icon, press and hold down the left mouse button and then move the mouse around. This allows you to 'carry' the file around using the mouse cursor. You can now 'drop' the file in a new location. If you release the left mouse button while the file is over the desktop it will be moved to your desktop. Drop it over a folder and it will be moved into the folder, drop the file onto a program icon and the program will start with that file loaded into it.

A variation on drag and drop can be performed if you use the right mouse button instead of the left. Remember we said that the right button opens up a context sensitive menu? Well the same happens when you drag and drop using the right button. Using the right button, drag and drop any file onto a folder and when you release the right button you will see a new menu open. This usually gives you four options – moving, copying, cancelling or creating a shortcut to the original file.

Drag and drop is not limited to Windows itself. You can use drag and drop within programs themselves and between Windows and programs that are currently running. One common example is dragging a selection of text to a new position. To do this, hold the left mouse button down and drag the mouse over the text you want to move, this text will now be highlighted. You can move the text by placing the cursor over the text, holding the left mouse button down, and 'dragging' the cursor to where you want the text to go. Want to save a section of text from a document as a separate file? Highlight the text and drag it onto the desktop, where it will appear as a new file.

Absolute Beginners:
the start menu

Once Windows is installed on your PC, it's no longer 'empty'. If you know where to look, you'll find useful applications to enable you to work quicker and easier with your PC

Start Menu

Complete newcomers to computing often wonder where to begin when faced with a computer screen. Since the introduction of Windows 95, the answer has been staring us in the face – it's the Start button. You'll normally find it at the bottom-left in the grey-coloured taskbar; and if you hover the mouse over it you'll see the tool-tip message "Click here to begin". When you click the Start Button, the Start Menu opens. Notice that some of the items listed have a right-pointing arrowhead. This means that there is a further flyout menu from that item.

When you highlight Programs, the flyout menu has Accessories at the top which also has a right-pointing arrowhead, indicating another flyout menu. You may like to see what's on offer in the Games group when you have time. Meanwhile, for this example, we'll go to the last item in the list – WordPad. Having selected and highlighted this option, click on it to open the WordPad application.

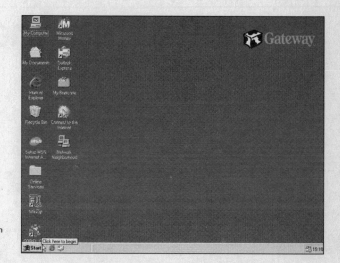

The Start button is tucked at the bottom left

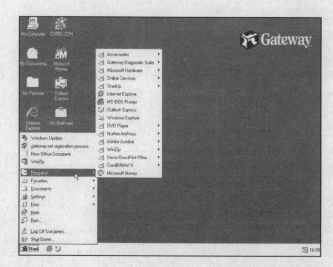

Arrowheads on the right indicate a flyout menu

Absolute Beginners:
using the taskbar

The Start Menu lies at the heart of Windows, so it's a good idea to get to know it. Here we look at running programs from it

The Start Menu displays a list of crucial items pertaining to the running of your computer, and one you will probably visit more often than others will be the Programs folder. This lets you start any program you see on the list. Most programs put themselves on the Programs list, so you will always know where to find them. We show you how to run an item from here and, also, we look at the taskbar.

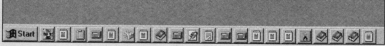

If too many applications are opened at the same time on your computer, the taskbar will not be able to accommodate all the buttons which show what functions are available to the user. A small up and down arrow icon then appears which will let you view parts of the list that are not currently visible.

If you work with a large number of windows open, increase the thickness of the taskbar so that it can display more buttons. Do this by passing the mouse over the top edge of the bar until the pointer changes to a double-headed arrow. Click the mouse and then drag the upwards to the desired size.

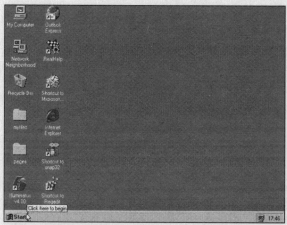

1 **Locate the Start button** Move your mouse pointer over the Start button, located in the bottom-left corner of the screen on the taskbar, and left-click. A menu will now appear above the Start button, containing links to other menus.

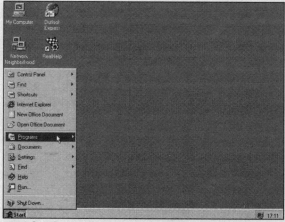

2 **Go to Programs** Move the mouse pointer to the item marked Programs – as soon as the pointer is above this a new menu will appear. (Note: menus with an arrow have another menu attached to them).

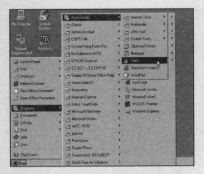

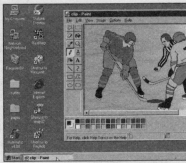

3 **Searching for Paint** Now move the mouse pointer across and up to the Accessories folder. When another menu appears, move your pointer across and down to the Paint option and left mouse click on it in order to select it.

4 **A change to the taskbar** The application you have selected, e.g. Paint, will now start. Notice the taskbar at the bottom now has a button. This button allows you to switch between programs when you have more than one running.

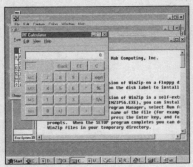

5 **Use the taskbar** You can demonstrate the benefits of using the taskbar by simply opening several applicationsor documents from the Start menu. Every time you open a file, it is represented by a button on the taskbar.

6 **Overlapping windows** As each application opens, its particular window overlays others that are already open. You can use a particular window's button on the taskbar to bring the application you want to work on to the front of the pile.

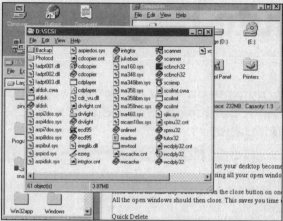

7 **Minimise all windows** If, with all the open application windows, the desktop starts getting a bit untidy, you can quickly tidy the desktop area by right clicking on a blank area of the taskbar and choosing the 'Minimise All Windows' option.

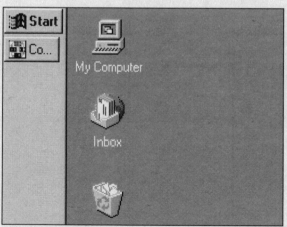

8 **Move the taskbar** You don't have to accept the default Taskbar position. To move the Taskbar to a new position, click and hold on a blank area of the Taskbar and move the pointer towards the chosen screen edge.

Absolute Beginners:
run a program

Not all of the programs on your computer appear on the Start Menu, but luckily there is a quicker method of running them

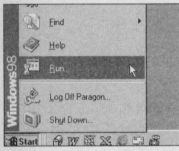

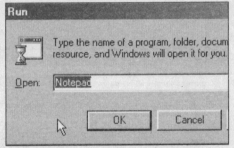

1 To begin, you need to left-click the mouse on the Start button in order to get access to the menu and then move the mouse pointer up to Run. Now left-click the mouse button to bring the Run dialog box up on the screen.

2 Move the pointer to the box marked Open, click the left mouse button inside the box. Now type in the name of the item you wish to run. This can be a program, folder, document or an Internet site. Note: you can access a folder within a folder by separating the folder names by a slash when you type them in.

You will no doubt have noticed that not all of the programs on your computer appear on the main Start Menu and can only be accessed by clicking your way through numerous other menus. As this process can sometimes become tiresome, there is a feature, fortunately, that can help you access programs and other items that are not otherwise instantly available. This feature is known as the Run command, and simply by entering the name of the program in question and clicking OK, you can access it immediately without having to locate and open it manually. Certain applications cannot be opened by Run (in

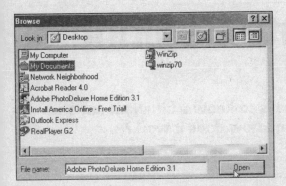

3 If you don't know the exact name of the item that you want to run, you should click on the Browse button in order to find it. Note that items recently opened by Run are displayed in the drop-down list.

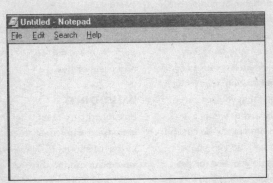

4 When you have entered the name of the item you want to run, simply click the OK button. Your chosen folder, program, document or Web site will then be opened up with a minimum amount of fuss.

particular external components installed via CD-ROMs), but the majority of basic Windows utility programs will be fine. Another useful feature of Run is that it can open Web pages directly, provided that you know the Internet address, which saves you the trouble of having to plough through Internet Explorer or your Netscape equivalent.

By using the Run command, you can also access a folder within another folder by typing the name of the path into the space next to 'open'. Starting with the letter of the drive and followed by the folder names, you will need to separate each with a slash. For example: c:/my documents/PC Home.

Absolute Beginners:
cut and paste

As a beginner, it pays to know a bit about cut and paste. What is it and how does it work?

Computers are designed to make our lives easier and, although they occasionally do the exact opposite, there are many situations where our PCs are a great help. Cutting and pasting is one area that will most definitely help you speed up certain tasks and allow you to do a whole range of things that would otherwise take an age to complete.

As you may have guessed, cutting and pasting is the process of taking one item from somewhere and placing it somewhere else – like cutting out a block of text from a newspaper and pasting it into a scrapbook. But computers, being the versatile things that they are, can do more than just cut and paste; you can also copy items. Instead of permanently cutting out a block of text you can copy it and then paste it to a new area in the same way.

When it comes to cutting and pasting, pretty much anything you see on your desktop or within a document can be cut and pasted. So files, icons, sections of text (or even single letters) and images can all be cut and pasted, or copied for that matter.

Before looking at the different things you can cut and paste, let's first take a look at how you go about the task itself. Essentially it's a three-step process:
1. You select the item you want to copy or cut;
2. You perform the action;
3. You choose where the item should go and then paste it.

There are three distinct ways in which you can perform these cut, copy and paste stages.

Keyboard

Possibly the quickest way is to use the universal keyboard shortcuts. These have been around for years and work across different computer platforms. The three keys involved are X, C and V.

Ctrl+X Cut
Ctrl+C Copy
Ctrl+V Paste

Menu

The next way is to use the standard menu system. Once you have selected the item you want, the Edit menu will give you access to the Cut, Copy and Paste options. Any options that are unavailable (for one reason or another) will be ghosted out.

Right-click

The final way involves the mouse and is easier than using the menu bar,

although some programs do not support it. Once you've selected the item you want to cut or copy simply right-click it and select the action you want from the menu that appears. To paste, just right-click the place where you want your cut or copied item to go.

When you perform a cut or copy, Windows calls

into play something known as the clipboard – a special storage area where Windows can temporarily keep cut or copied information. This area can only store a single piece of information so if you cut or copy something else, the previous item is erased. Unitil you do though, you can paste this item in as much as you like.

Special Cases

Cutting and pasting text and graphics are two things that you'll do with regularity. However the cut and paste feature is not limited to just this. Depending on the programs you use, you can cut and paste various things. Usually, if you can select it, you can copy and paste it.

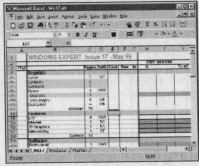

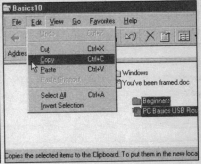

If you work with spreadsheets, you might be interested to discover that the cells that make up a worksheet can be copied and pasted wherever you like. You can also copy entire rows and columns by using the end buttons to select them and then use your copy and paste abilities

All your files and folders are open to copying and pasting. Just select one or as many as you like, select Cut to move them or Copy to duplicate. You then navigate to where you want the files to go and select Paste. The files are then automatically moved around your hard drive – easy as pie

Using Text

Manipulating text is probably one of the most common uses for the cut and paste function. You will be able to copy or cut letters, words and large chunks of text and then paste this back into the same document or even a totally different one if you like.

You should also bear in mind that this action is not only limited to documents. You will be able cut and paste text anywhere within Windows or within any program in which you can select items.

So, this means that file names and text boxes, for example, can also be cut and pasted. The options are almost endless.

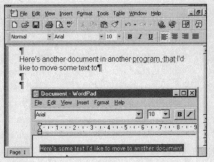

1 I have two different wordprocessors running, each with its own separate document. I want to move a selection of text from one to the other. The first step is to highlight the text I want to copy by holding down the left mouse button and moving the mouse cursor over the text. With the text selected, I can now perform the copy or cut. Use cut to move the text while if you want to repeat or duplicate text use the copy function.

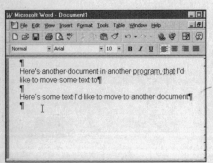

2 I will use one of the techniques described earlier, the simplest is to press Ctrl+C to copy or Ctrl+X to cut. I also have the option of using the Edit menu and selecting Cut or Copy from there. If the particular program supports it, you could also right-click the mouse and use the context sensitive menu. Now I can simply select the other wordprocessor's document and paste in the text, either by using the menu or by pressing Ctrl+V.

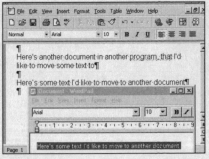

3 Text can also be pasted (you don't need to copy it again as it's still stored in the clipboard) into the name of a folder. To do this you need to create a new folder and then perform the paste action – your text will now become the name of the new folder. In the same way if you have a text box in another window you can copy and paste text information into this, handy for entering long registration numbers and the like.

Using Graphics

When it comes to copying and pasting graphics, things are slightly more complicated. The process is essentially the same as for text – you just select the area of a picture you want to copy and then paste this area elsewhere, either into the same picture or into another. The difference here is how you select the area to copy in the first place.

1 All paint packages, even the basic Paint that comes with Windows, allow you to specify rectangular regions of a picture. With the selection tool active, just left-click and drag the mouse cursor over the area that you would like to copy. Then, once you have released the button, you will then be left with a square showing you the area which you have selected – a little more complicated than selecting text.

2 If you then select Copy and then Paste, you should find that you have an exact duplicate of the selected area which you can then move around. Then, (if you carefully move the cursor to the edge of the region), you can resize it. If, on the other hand, you want to actually cut the region that you have chosen, you can simply start dragging it. This will then leave a blank area underneath where it was originally placed.

3 Some paint packages will work a little bit differently from others and many offer additional tools to make selecting areas to cut out or copy that much easier. Even the very basic Paint gives you a freehand selection tool which will help you when it comes to drawing around objects. But some other, better, packages will offer 'magic wands' that can actually select an area according to its colour.

Absolute Beginners:
Windows navigation

We take a close look at standard Windows programs and show you how to get to grips with the various features and functions

All Windows programs actually work in a similar way. So, it might come as no surprise to you to learn that if you know how to open and save a file with one program, then you can do it for all programs. In the same way, if you can use one menu, then you can use them all.

In this chapter, we are going to take a look at a standard Windows program called WordPad. Go to the Start Menu and select Programs/ Accessories/ WordPad.

The first thing you should notice is that it looks pretty similar to all the other windows.

There is the program's title bar at the top that has some caption buttons in the top right, the menu strip is there and, at the bottom, is the status bar. Just under the menu strip is a toolbar. Many programs make use of these, and they give you a shortcut to a programs that are commonly used functions.

It is possible to move toolbars to different positions. By dragging the left or right edge of the toolbar, you can move it to the top. bottom, left or right of the WordPad window. The toolbar can also be left floating over the main window – this last feature can be quite useful if you are working on higher resolution screens.

It isn't always convenient to have to grab the mouse if you just want to open a menu or click a button, so Windows gives you the option to use the keyboard to activate buttons, tabs and text gadgets. **Note:** With all these navigation tips, holding down the Shift key reverses the direction.

Access the menus by pressing Alt and the letter that is underlined in the menu's title. Once the menu is open, use the cursor keys to move the highlighted menu around.

Once a button has been highlighted with the faint ringed dotted line, you can then activate the button by just pressing the Return key.

If a button or tick box has an underlined letter (see picture below), you can press Alt and the letter to select it. Some other useful hints include:

Tab – To cycle through all the various buttons and text gadgets in a window, use the tab key. A faint dotted line will circle the currently selected button, use the Tab key to move this on.

Ctrl+Tab – Will cycle through the tabs in a window. If the tabs name is ringed, you can also use the cursor keys.

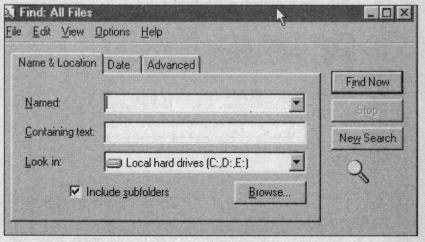

Absolute Beginners:
anatomy of a program

We take a closer look at the anatomy of a program – that is, the various different components which make up the program that you see on your screen

Title Bar

Almost every program has one. The title bar runs across the top of the window and contains the program's name and usually the title of the document you are working on. Use the title bar to move windows around the screen by left-clicking and holding the title bar and dragging the window to a new position. You can also fill the screen with the window by double-clicking the title bar, double-click again to return the window to its normal size.

Menu

The menu strip on every window lives directly under the title bar. Each word in the menu strip lets you access a whole new selection of options by left-clicking it once. Put the mouse cursor over the one you want and click it.

Toolbar

Many programs have additional toolbars that run underneath the main menu strip. These contain the most commonly used tools and functions which you can access with a single mouse click. You'll also find that many programs (but not WordPad) let you customise these so you can have the tools you want. This is usually done through the Edit/Preference or Tool/Customise menus.

Scroll Bar

If you are editing a document larger than the program window you'll need a way of moving the document around. Do this by using the scroll bars and scroll buttons, You can left-click the scroll buttons to shift the document around in single steps. To move in larger amounts left-click and hold the scroll bar.

Palette Toolbar

Floating toolbars are called palettes. If you left-click and hold the left end of a toolbar under the menu strip and drag it over the main document area you'll find that when you release the mouse button it turns into a little window, or palette; it's just another way of having toolbars on screen. To turn a palette back into a toolbar, you have to "dock" it back under the menu strip – left-click and hold any blank area of the palette, drag it to the menu strip and release.

Document Area

The largest part of any program is the main document area. Its appearance varies depending on the job the program has to do. A wordprocessor has a text cursor that you can move around the document and use to insert text and an art package has a blank canvas onto which you can paint. Each new piece of software you use will involve you learning some new techniques.

Buttons:

Clicking on this closes the current window. If the window happens to be a program or document, it will close as well.

Windows can be used in two different modes – full screen and resizable. This button can be used to switch the screen between the two.

The minimise button hides the current window from view. In order to restore a window, you need to click on its button in the taskbar.

Absolute Beginners:
shut down

Why can't I just switch off my computer? The simple answer is you can, but it's definitely not advisable. We explain why using shut down is the best way to switch off your PC

Windows 95 and 98 store operating files on a small section of your hard disk and Windows actually controls your machine as long as it is switched on. When you want to switch off your PC, you need to give Windows the chance to erase these files, tidy up and also make sure that all the files are in order for next time.

To do this, a simple shut down procedure has to be followed that only takes a few seconds. Not performing this routine will leave files lying open all over your hard disk, making them exposed to the chance of loss and when you come to use the computer again you may find faults have occurred and you cannot open a file that you could previously. Your PC will more than likely perform 'Scandisk,' an operation designed to check everything is in place on your system. This takes time, whereas shutting down will prevent that and any unwanted viruses as well.

Here's a step-by-step guide to shutting down.

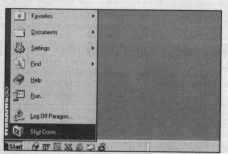

1 When you are ready to end a Windows session, left-click the Start button and then select Shut Down from the menu. The screen will become darker and an option menu will appear.

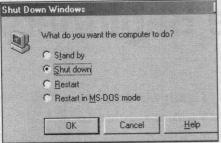

2 The menu will give you the option to shut down or restart the computer in either Windows or DOS mode. You also get the chance to escape the shutting down sequence and carry on with your Windows session. To do this, click the Cancel button. To shut down, click in the circle by the Shut down option, then click OK.

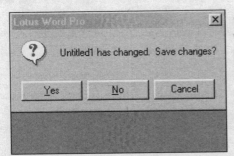

3 In the event that Windows detects an unsaved file, which it will if you were working on something just prior to shutting down and forgot to save it, this dialog box will appear onscreen. It will give you the option to either save changes to your document or abandon it for good. Simply choose either Yes or No at this point to either save the file or lose it completely.

4 After a few seconds of hard disk activity, Windows will have erased its operating files from the hard disk and saved its configuration files ready for the next session. A screen will appear that will say something similar to 'Please wait while your computer shuts down.' A few seconds later your machine will automatically switch itself off leaving you to remember to turn off your monitor.

It's now safe to turn off your computer.

Absolute Beginners:
buttons/saving files

There's a whole world of gadgets and buttons out there. Here's a quick guide to what they all do

As you become a little more proficient when using your PC and begin to tackle more programs, you will come across many different types of gadgets and buttons. This chapter takes a look at some of these gadgets and what function(s) they carry out

Look in – If you know a file you are looking for is on a certain drive or in a certain folder, simply use this pull-down menu to move to that location quickly.

Up one level – If you click your way through a number of folders and want to return to the previous one, click this button to take you back up a folder level.

Desktop – The desktop as a handy place to store files and documents. If you want to switch to see the files on your desktop, click this button.

New folder – If you are starting a new project, you may want to keep all the files in a particular folder; to make a new folder you can simply click this button.

Files of type – This pull-down menu lets you filter the different types of file that are displayed in the dialog box. So if you are only interested in Word documents you can select these here, or if you want to be able to see every type of file you can select the relevant option. If you are saving a file, use this menu to pick what file format the program should use.

Open/Cancel – Once you've selected the file you want to open you can either just double-click it or select it then click the Open button. To dismiss the dialog box, simply click on Cancel.

View type – These two buttons let you alter the type of view the dialog box uses to display the files in a folder. One is a plain list while the other shows you precise details about each file.

Tabs – To help simplify things, many windows you use will be split into sections and the named tabs at the top of the window let you jump between these sections. Just click them to bring that particular section to the front.

Pull down menu – These are used to let you select a single option from a long list of possibilities. The currently selected one is displayed; to view the rest click the down arrow and scroll through the list that appears. Click the options you want.

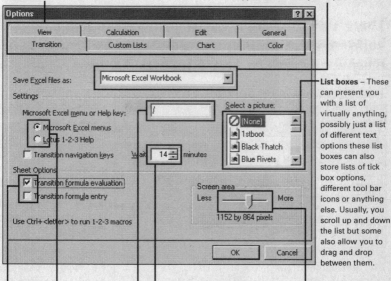

List boxes – These can present you with a list of virtually anything, possibly just a list of different text options these list boxes can also store lists of tick box options, different tool bar icons or anything else. Usually, you scroll up and down the list but some also allow you to drag and drop between them.

Radio buttons – These are named after the push buttons on a radio and represent options that are mutually exclusive. That means that only one can be active at a time; click one of the others and the currently selected item will be cleared.

Value boxes – Often, you'll have to enter a fixed value for an option and value boxes simplify the process. On the left side is the area where the value is inserted, while to the right you will usually see an up and down arrow. You can either type the value directly into the box, or use the arrows to increase or decrease the value.

Slider bars – These let you easily navigate documents that are larger than the window they are contained in and enable you to view each different part. These scroll bars are made up of a number of sections: Buttons that scroll a single step at a time, the scroll bar that lets you scroll the document an arbitrary amount and the blank area around the scroll area that enables you to scroll one page at a time.

Tick boxes – Just like in a questionnaire, tick boxes can be either clear or have a tick in place. They represent options that can be either on or off. Click the box to select the option and click again to clear the tick.

Text boxes – If you need to provide a program with a short text value, you'll need to use a text box. This is a small area into which you can type, copy, paste and cut text as you would with a word processor.

Absolute Beginners:
folders and files

There's a lot to learn when you start to use a computer but once you understand the basics, you'll discover it's not as mysterious as it seems

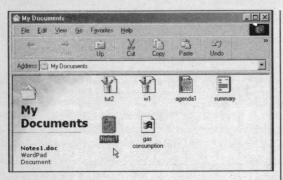

One problem new computer users often encounter (and one that even the most experienced occasionally meet) is in not knowing how to return to files they have saved. It's all too easy to imagine that a document or picture you worked on previously has been lost when all that has really

happened is that it's been filed in an unexpected location.

Windows is an 'object-oriented' computer system. In other words, it models what happens to real world objects in the virtual world of the computer. Therefore, it refers to any documents, pictures, spreadsheets and so on that you save as

'files' which are subsequently kept in what's called 'folders.'

The folders that you use most often can be kept on the computer's desktop but, alternatively, they can be kept hidden from initial view within the computer's filing system. As in the real world, if you place a file in the wrong folder, or the folder in the wrong drawer of the filing cabinet, it is lost for all practical purposes.

Unlike a paper document and a physical set of drawers, there are more efficient ways of finding missing files and folders on your computer and putting them back in their correct places.

Managing your files

Keeping everything in My Documents is the same as keeping all your documents in a single, undifferentiated heap and while this works well as long as you only have a few items to keep track of, you'll quickly need a system with more structure.

If you click on the My Computer icon on the desktop, you will see an icon labelled with the name of the computer's hard disk. It will normally end in C: and may even be plain, unadorned [C:].

A hard disk is the computer's filing system and unless your PC is part of a network, all the programs you use – as well as all your data – will be kept on it. It is usually a good idea to keep data in separate folders to programs and to create new sub-folders – folders within other folders – for each specific task.

For example, suppose you were to start writing a book using the word processor. You could create a new folder for the whole book and then create sub-folders within that folder in which you can store each subsequent chapter.

Creating a folder

Open your C: drive and right-click with the mouse on any white space you can find. Click on the last but one item in the menu that appears, New, and then select Folder from the very top of the sub-menu that opens. A folder called 'New Folder'

appears. The next step is to give it a name. If you do this immediately you'll notice that the name New Folder is highlighted in blue and anything you type will replace it. Windows 98 supports long names. Therefore, if you intend to create more than one book you can type in something meaningful (so you can find it easily at a later date) – here we have entered 'Book of Recipes.'

Click on the icon of the new folder and create more folders inside it – you could call them Chapter 1, Chapter 2 and so on. Here, we've used sections of the Recipe Book.

Selecting the option that allows you to create a brand new folder

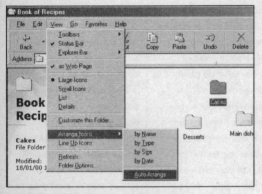

When you click on an empty space to create folders, they materialise at the point where you clicked and the result can soon become untidy. Move folders by dragging or arrange them using the command Arrange Icons.

Arranging the contents of a folder by name or by date often helps to find items you've lost. Just as in a real filing system, there are variable levels of nesting. Using our example of a cookery book project, Soups and Starters, Main dishes, Desserts and so on. The Main dishes folder has folders within it for Beef, Chicken, Vegetarian and so on. To get from one level of the hierarchy to another, there are two

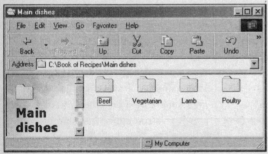

distinct methods. To open a folder within a folder, simply double-click with the mouse. To close it and climb back to the former level, you should use either the Up or Back button on the toolbar.

To rename a folder at a later time, you can use the right-click menu and select Rename. Or, you can single-click on the folder and then single-click on its label. If you double-click you will open the folder rather than select its name.

You might also decide to add a new level to the hierarchy. For example, you have recipes for Turkey and Duck. This suggests that you create a new folder Poultry and put the existing Chicken folder inside it. To do this simply drag the Chicken folder on top of the new Poultry folder. When you drag a folder, you should notice that it turns blue at its original position and only a shadowy yellow version travels with the cursor. When the destination folder into which you want to put it also turns blue, release the mouse button – you will have successfully moved the folder. You can move files into folders in exactly the same way.

Saving files

When you save a file in any application you'll usually be presented with a default filename and a default location. The location will often be My Documents or the last folder in which you saved a file of the same type. Sometimes, the proposed destination is sensible, other times it might be very inappropriate.

A good tip when creating a document from scratch – and always when modifying an existing one to produce something new – is to save the document as the very first step. In other words, save as soon as you begin even though it is just a blank spreadsheet or just a empty word processor page. The main reason for this is that having assigned a name and location, clicking the save icon will then save the latest changes to the same file, therefore allowing you to save often with minimum effort.

When you come to save a file, if you realise it also needs a new folder, use the New Folder icon in the Save As dialog box. First, move to the folder in which you want the folder creating. If, for example, you had already created the Poultry folder but not one for Chicken, double-click Main Dishes, then double-click Poultry so that it appears in the Save in box. Then click the New Folder Icon. A dialog appears in which you type the name of the new folder: Chicken, for instance. Next double-click the new Chicken folder to open it before finally clicking the Save button.

Creating new files

You will probably be familiar with how to create a new document from within an application but it's worth knowing that you can create, name and open files from the filing system.

Go to the folder where you want the new file and right-click on a empty area. Select New from the drop-down menu, then choose the appropriate type of file from the list. For example, choose Microsoft Word Document or Microsoft Excel Worksheet. Name the file and then double click on it to open the application concerned. Another way to create new files (or new folders) is to use the File command in the File Manager's menu bar. You'll find the New command in its drop-down list and it has exactly the same facilities for new folders and new files alike.

Renaming, moving and copying files

We have already seen how to rename folders and the same principle holds for files. Right-click on the file's icon and then select Rename from the pop-up menu. Or you can single-click on the file and then click again on its name label. Either way, the label is highlighted in blue while the file icon itself is not highlighted. Now simply type in the name you want.

Moving a file between folders can be done in three ways – by dragging, using the right click menu or using keyboard short cuts. To use dragging you need to be able to see the file and its new destination at the same time. For example, here you could drag the file Casseroles into Main Dishes but not into the Chicken folder, which is inside Poultry which is, in turn, inside Main Dishes.

An alternative method is to use the Cut command in this folder, then move to the destination folder (by double-clicking to open Main Dishes, double-clicking again to open the Poultry folder and again to open Chicken), then Paste in the file. Cut is found on the right click menu and its shortcut is Ctrl-X, which works when the file is selected (or highlighted). Paste appears on the right click whenever there is something (in this case a file) available to be pasted and the shortcut is Ctrl-V.

Similarly, there are three ways to copy. You can use Copy from the right-click menu, or its shortcut instead, Ctrl-C, followed by opening the desired destination folder and using Paste (Ctrl-V). Alternatively, if you drag a file with the Ctrl key held down you will notice that the original icon stays where it was and the shadowy new one has a + sign situated next to it.

If you drag the Casseroles' file to another place within the same folder you will see that the new file name is 'Copy of Casseroles'. If you drag it to another folder, its name will stay as Casseroles. This is perfectly acceptable. You can have a file called Casseroles inside the Beef folder, another one with the same name inside the Lamb folder and so on. This can cause confusion if taken to extremes – for example, if you call all your letter files 'Letter' and rely on having folders for all the correspondents you may lose documents when you forget people's names. Perhaps it would be better to have a folder for letters and use the name of the recipient as the filenames.

QuickView

An alternative method of viewing your files is to use the Windows QuickView utility. QuickView is not actually installed in a typical Windows installation from the CD-ROM supplied. In order to add it, double-click on Add/Remove Programs in the Control Panel folder, select the Windows Setup tab and then follow the onscreen instructions. QuickView is a component of Accessories.

You have now seen how you can modify your filing system and impose a logical structure on it. You have also seen how you can create folders and files within the File Manager and noted that there are facilities for creating folders available in the Save As dialog in applications such as a word processor. Get used to taking advantage of these to maintain an ordered system so you always know where your files are!

The My Documents folder

The My Documents folder is kept on the desktop. Clicking on its icon on the desktop will open the folder and let you inspect its contents.

Address box shows full details of the folders within folders

Use the Up arrow to move higher up the folder hierarchy

Click on this arrow to access a drop-down list of all locations

The File menu is an alternative way to create a New file

Different icons are used for files according to their type. For example, bitmap files are indicated by a jar of pencils and markers, while text and document files have a notebook icon

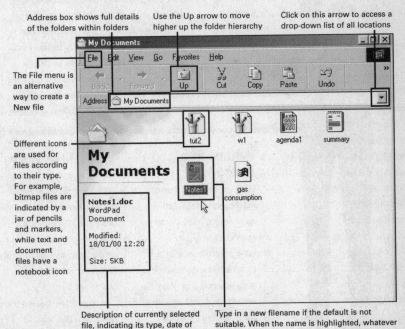

Description of currently selected file, indicating its type, date of last editing, size and other details

Type in a new filename if the default is not suitable. When the name is highlighted, whatever you type will instantly overwrite existing text

Absolute Beginners:
finding lost files

This part of our Absolute Beginners' Guide takes a look at how you can recover files and folders which you think you might have lost

It's very easy to imagine that a document or picture has been deleted and lost forever when all that's happened is it's been misnamed or misfiled.

As we've seen already in this book, you can create a logical filing system on your computer in order to keep track of your data files. In that chapter, we concentrated on creating folders and files. This time we'll look at the information provided in a file's name and the facilities on offer for finding files when they have gone missing.

What's in a name?

Until recently, whatever application you were working in, a file name was restricted to eight letters/numbers with a three-letter extension. It is only recently that long file names, with more flexible rules, such as spaces between words, have been allowed and you may still have some older programs that demand you conform to the strict set of rules that pre-date 32-bit applications. It also explains the rather cryptic names you may find if you explore data from a few years ago.

It is worth knowing that programs that do not support long file names will

Microsoft Word

The file name, location, or format 'Characters not permitted:' is not valid. Type the file name and location in the correct format, such as c:\location\file name.

OK

The message that appears when there's a colon in a proposed filename

not allow you to use spaces or hyphens in names but do permit the underscore character.

Long filenames can be up to 255 characters – but this allocation is for the file's full address – which also includes its immediate folder and then all the other folders going back to the drive letter. It's conceivable that if you assign long folder names and lots of nesting in the filing hierarchy you might come close to the limit – but, on the whole, it is fairly unlikely.

The other main restriction is that file names cannot include any of the following characters:
forward slash – /
backslash – \
greater than sign – >
less than sign – <
asterisk – *
question mark – ?
quotation mark – "
pipe symbol – |
colon – :
semicolon – ;

What happens when you try to use these characters varies depending on the meaning that Windows attaches to the symbol and the program you are using.

A question mark or asterisk causes Word not to respond at all as they mean that information is missing, while a forward or backslash produces a message to the effect that a folder isn't accessible since slashes are used as the separators between folder names. The normal response is an onscreen message telling you that the name you have typed in is not valid and to try an alternative.

File extensions

The full stop (.) is also included in the list of proscribed characters and, while programs seem to allow it, it is best to avoid it. This is because it's the character used between the file name that the user supplies and the three letter file extension that is automatically added to designate the type of file.

File types used to be something that all computer users had to know about because they were not added by programs, but these days its easier to ignore them – which is fine until your data goes missing.

Using the Files and Folders window

One of the commonest reasons for files going missing is file management itself! Most applications give you an easy way to open the most recently worked on files – you will normally see a list when you use the File, Open command – and you can open documents and launch their appropriate applications from the Windows Start menu.

If in between creating the file and wanting to use it again you've engaged in a filing session, you may well be responsible for the file going missing. Perhaps you really have deleted an unwanted version or maybe you have created a new folder and moved the existing file into it. Equally, if you have renamed the folder or nested inside another one then Windows will not be able to find it and you need to look for it yourself.

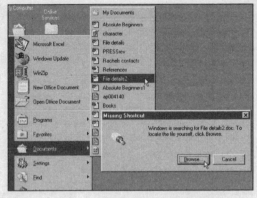

Here we've tried to launch Microsoft Word with a recently used file that has since been disturbed by file maintenance

If you click Browse in this situation, you'll be taken to Word's Open dialog box – but this is not necessarily the best place to start looking. Instead, click My Computer on the desktop and navigate through your directory structure as discussed in last month's article.

Keep your clock right

The date on which a file was modified can be so useful in locating missing files it is, therefore, important to keep your computer's clock absolutely right. It's so easy to do there's no excuse. Simply double click on the time shown in the System Tray (or right-click on it and select Adjust Date/Time from the menu that appears) to open the Date/Time Properties dialog box. Here, choose the correct date from its calendar display and enter the time in the box under the clock display.

Wildcard

When you type into the Named: box you can ignore the file extension. For example, if you type in "test" the resulting list may contain test.doc, test.txt, test.xls, test.pcx and so on. On the other hand, you may be able to use the file extension to help you find a file. For example, if you use Excel and have saved a spreadsheet whose name you cannot remember then searching for *.xls (or better still for *.xl? which will find spreadsheets saved using one of the allowable file variations. (The wildcard character ? stands in place of a single character so .xl? is matched by .xls, .xlt, .xlw and other Excel extensions).

In the case of a Word document, a shadowy icon and a filename preceded by ˜$ normally denotes that the file is already open

Click here to cycle through four alternative views – this view is Large Icons

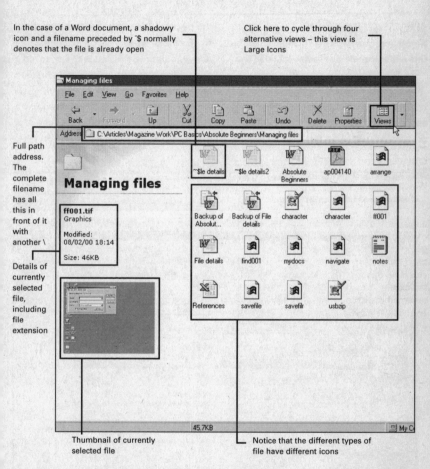

Full path address. The complete filename has all this in front of it with another \

Details of currently selected file, including file extension

Thumbnail of currently selected file

Notice that the different types of file have different icons

The Files and Folders window has more information than you are normally aware of to help you. For a start, make sure you read the entry in the Address box. This gives the first part of every file in the folder's name. So the complete name of the document we've just tried to open is:
C:\Articles\Magazine Work\PC Basics\Absolute Beginners\Managing files\File details2 (which is 84 characters long if you count spaces!).

Viewing your files

There are four ways in which files can be viewed in the My Computer folders. The default is Large Icons, if you choose Small Icons, files are arranged in four columns across the page with their names to the right of the each icon. List re-arranges the same information down the page while Details view, as here, has the Size and Type of each file and the date and time at which it was last saved – this information can be located in the Modified column.

Sorting the list of files using Modified is a good way to find a file if you can remember when you last worked on it.

The Main View menu has commands for four variants on display and clicking Arrange Icons has four ways of sorting

Click here to arrange icons interactively

Notice that the size of the corrupt file is just 1K compared to 59K for the undamaged File details file

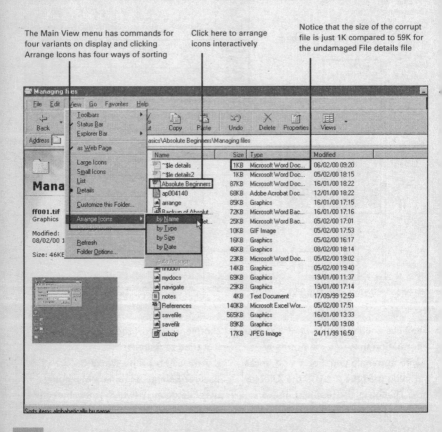

Using dates

If you select the between option in order to find files, you can type in the dates or select them from a drop-down calendar.

We've already seen that the date of a file's latest modification is stored as part of the details that you can view. The Date section of the Find dialog allows you to use date information to narrow your search. By default it is set to All files, but if you know when you most recently modified the file (or when you created it or last accessed it), you can restrict the search to a range of dates or simply to a recent period. In this case, you can set either the number of months or of days.

The need for backup

Losing files is something that all computer users will experience at one time or another. If your machine crashes while you are using a word processor, then you may be lucky in that the application will be able to recover the latest auto save.

Even so, though, there are several scenarios that lead to users leaving an application without saving their work properly. It is important then, that you practice regularly backing up your files and documents, that way, if your computer crashes, you will still have your important documents backed up.

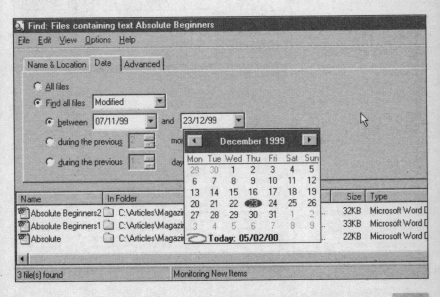

Using Find

The Find command is on the start menu. Clicking it opens a flyout menu. Choose Files or Folder to open this dialog box.

If you know file name, or the part of the name, you are but have no idea where it is stored then just type the part you are confident about, with wild card characters to indicate the missing bits, into the Named: box. For example abs* means a filename starting abs followed by some (or none) other characters, while *2 means any number of characters with 2 at the very end of the name. You can even use the asterisk twice as in *beginner*.

An alternative, when you can't remember what you called the file but can remember a distinctive word or phrase that you typed into it, is to use the Containing text: box.

There are two potential problems, though, with these two searches – if you have a lot of files then this search can take a long time. If you choose a partial name that can be completed in many different ways, or a phrase that could crop up in lots of contexts, then the resulting list can be quite long.

One way to restrict the search is to instruct the computer where to look. In this case I know that my files are saved on drive C inside a folder called Magazine Work which, in turn, is inside a folder called Articles.

Remember you can also use the browse button to widen the search. For instance, could you have saved a file on the hard disk (the C drive) when you intended it to be stored on a floppy diskette in A:?

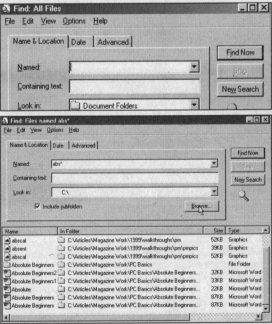

Using the * wildcard to search for filenames beginning with abs

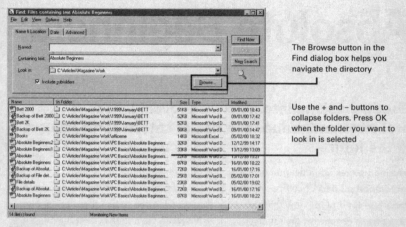

The Browse button in the Find dialog box helps you navigate the directory

Use the + and – buttons to collapse folders. Press OK when the folder you want to look in is selected

File types

Although the way that files and folders work is fairly simple there are one or two mysteries that might have you puzzled without a word or two of explanation. For example, how does your PC know what type a file is? After all it seems to know when you create a word processing file or a graphic file because it uses different icons for each one. It also usually manages to associate files with their correct application program. How does it do this? The answer is that file types are indicated by a three letter 'extension' at the end of every file name. For instance, when you use a word processor to create a document called MyFile it is

actually called MyFile.doc or something similar. When you use a graphics program to create a document with the same name it is in fact called MyFile.tif. The actual ending used depends on the file's type and which program created it.

Most of the time you will be unaware of this use of extensions because they aren't shown. When you see the contents of a folder the file types are indicated by the icons used and the extension is hidden. Most of the time this works well but if you do want to see the three letter extensions use the folder command View, Options and then select the View tab in the dialog box that appears.

Make sure that the 'Hide file extensions for known files' option is un-ticked. After this you will see all file extensions but be careful not to change an extension unless you mean to because that will change the file type and its association with the application that created it.

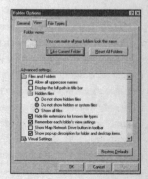

Absolute Beginners:
disk maintenance

Routine disk maintenance can reveal a host of problems and reduce the risk of catastrophic failures in the future

Backing up files and documents is a very important part of computing. It is important for you to know that the hard drive's Properties dialog, in addition to a backup facility, offers error checking as well as defragmentation utilities.

In this chapter, we'll consider when and how often to use these tools. First, however, we'll look at everyday disk maintenance chores including deleting unwanted files and programs.

Dealing with a full disk

If you have a fairly new computer, the chances are that it has a large hard disk and you'll only use a small proportion of it – at first. It is, however, amazing how quickly a hard disk can fill and a disk that seemed huge initially can seem puny only a few months later. Having a disk that is almost full doesn't just present the problem of how to fit the next program or data you want to store, it also slows down applications that are already installed because they have to hunt for room to accommodate their temporary files. So, if your computer starts to run slow the first remedy is to discover whether your disk is clogged.

Place a tick against the types of files you want to remove

Hard disk Properties

To open a hard disk's Properties box, right-click on its icon in My Computer and select Properties. The General Tab displays the Capacity of the disk with the proportion used in blue and the free space in magenta. Notice that there's also a button for Disk Cleanup, which can often free up a few precious megabytes by emptying the Recycle Bin and also deleting temporary Internet files, downloaded program files and other temporary files.

Temporary Internet files

If you are an active user of the Internet you may be surprised by just how much disk space is taken up by temporary Internet files. These files will have accumulated on your disk to speed up viewing Web sites you have visited. If you use the View Files button you will probably notice that a large proportion of the files are for graphics objects. You can safely delete all such files without any knock-on effects to applications that you

use but you may notice slow operation next time you surf the Internet. If you regularly visit the same Web sites is worth inspecting the list of files that would be deleted. Bear in mind that you can manually delete unwanted files rather than opt for the wholesale deletion of all of them using the Disk Cleanup.

Downloading files

Downloaded program files also refers to Internet-related content – this time routines needed to make certain Web pages 'perform.' They are often used for animations and other graphics effects. Again, if you regularly visit pages that need these files it isn't sensible to delete them but the worst that will happen is that you have to re-download and re-install programs such as Shockwave.

As long as you have saved all your work-in-progress and exited applications such as your word processor and spreadsheet before going ahead with Disk Cleanup, there should be no problems with deleting temporary files – but, in general, they will not account for much disk space. If they do, it suggests something is wrong with your system since temporary files are the ones kept by applications as part of their automatic recovery procedures and are normally deleted instantly at the end of a work session.

Clean your disk

You may find that Disk Cleanup doesn't free up much space and decide to explore More Options. Two of the options, Windows components and Installed programs open the Add/Remove Programs dialog box. You may have met this

The various options available to you when you opt for a Disk Cleanup

before in the context of installing programs and via a different route, because another way to open this dialog is via the Control Panel which you can access by clicking on the Settings option in the Start menu. When inspecting your Windows Setup with a view to cleaning up your disk, look for items that take up disk space but are not entirely necessary.

For example, Desktop Themes is a good candidate for removal if it is installed as it accounts for over 30Mb and is a frivolous extra rather than actually being central to the operation of any programs.

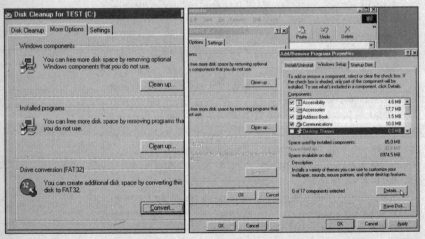

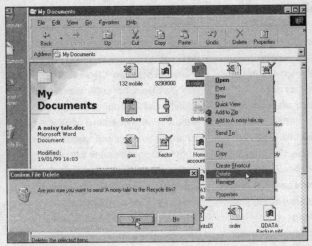

required. If the unwanted file is in a folder elsewhere in the filing system you can still drag it to the Recycle Bin just resize the directory window so that the Bin is visible at the same time. If the Recycle Bin is hidden, you can click on the icon of the file you want to delete and use the command Delete on the File menu or simply press the Del key.

Deleting files

There are various ways of deleting files and the most important thing to know is that just giving the command Delete doesn't necessarily get rid of the file irrevocably when you are using Windows 95 or 98. Files that you delete are placed into the Recycle Bin and it is only when you empty it that your files can be considered lost and gone. Even after this, remnants of a file can remain and can sometimes be retrieved by a good deal of effort on the part of an expert. This raises security issues that we won't go into here, but for all normal purposes once files have been emptied out of the Recycle Bin you should consider them irretrievable.

So, how should you get rid of unwanted files? If the file in question is on the desktop you can simply drag it to the Recycle Bin. You will see a 'Confirm File Delete' message asking if you are sure and you should click on Yes if the file concerned is no longer

If you want to avoid the step of storing an unwanted file in the Recycle Bin then pressing Shift at the same time as giving the Delete command removes it from your disk in a single step. This leads to a different message that asks if you are sure you want to delete the file. There's no second chance when you use this method so only use it when you really are sure.

Click and install

A tick beside an item indicates it is installed (and a tick on a grey background indicates part of a component is installed). To regain disk space, click on an installed item so that its tick disappears. You will also see space freed up appear in red.

The Details button can be used not only to find out more about a component but also to make more choices. For example you can select a specific Desktop Theme but remove others you are not interested in.

Clicking the Clean up button in the Installed programs section of More Options takes you to the Install/Uninstall section of Add/Remove Programs where you will see a list of programs that can be removed if you wish.

Obviously, you should only remove programs you don't need on a regular basis and it is worth looking for items that take up a substantial amount of disk space and are not going to be a lot of trouble to reinstall if you

want them again in future.

Highlight one that you want to remove and you'll see a Confirm File Deletion box that checks that you really do want to delete the program. Click Yes. The Windows Uninstall utility then loads. Sometimes it will complete its task without further questions but if it detects certain types of file associated with a program UninstallShield will request confirmation before it removes them. The files concerned are ones that can be shared by other programs and so UninstallShield cannot be sure that removing them won't have consequences for programs you want to retain. When you see a message like this one, the safest option is to choose 'No to all' since you too cannot be sure if removing a shared file will affect other programs.

It's worth knowing that you can use Ctrl+A to select all the files in a folder. If you wanted to exclude a specific file from the selection, then hold down the Ctrl key and click on the file name or its icon.

The final option in Disk Cleanup is Drive Conversion – an option that will be unavailable if your disk already is a FAT32 disk. As disk sizes have increased Windows has had to use different methods of keeping track of the space. The original method was called FAT16 but it can't handle very large disks. FAT 32 was introduced to allow Windows to work with larger disks but converting a FAT 16 disk to FAT 32 can increase the amount of storage space on your disk. The only problem with doing this when your disk is very full is that it would be advisable to back up valuable data first as the procedure is not risk-free! There are situations in which you should stick with your existing disk – mainly to do with compatibility if you ever remove your hard drive and take it to a different system – so click to read the details of the conversion process.

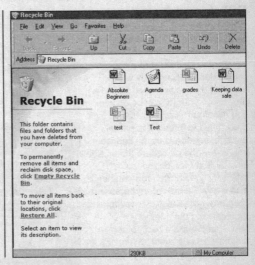

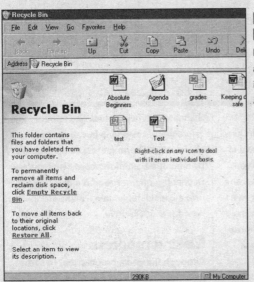

Right-click on any icon to deal with it on an individual basis.

Inspecting the Recycle Bin

Back on the desktop you can see, at a glance, whether there is anything in the Recycle Bin – any contents appear as crumpled paper.

Right-clicking on the Recycle Bin's icon will bring up a pop-up menu that allows you to Open the Recycle Bin just like any other folder and you should do this before emptying it just to make sure files or folders haven't been placed in it by mistake. In the picture on the left, you can see what your Recycle Bin folder actually looks like.

Defragmentation

If you have a large hard disk and it is nearly full then defragmentation is going to take a considerable time. By its very nature this is not a chore that can be done concurrently with anything else so you need to find a time when your PC can be on without you needing to use it. However, even if you have to interrupt it, partial defragmentation is useful and when you restart the procedure the portion already done will be repeated relatively quickly. Defragmentation is also a low-risk procedure because the program moves files by copying and then deleting the original – even so, you should make a backup of anything you consider valuable.

Defragmentation is very worthwhile – you will notice that a disk that had been very sluggish is restored to a much more acceptable performance. This is because while formerly it took it a long time to actually find a suitable space to write data, there is now one large free area which files can be stored in.

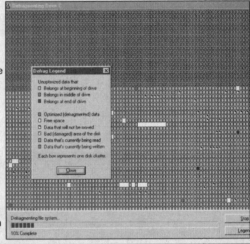

Checking with ScanDisk

Many PCs will automatically run ScanDisk for you if your machine isn't shut down in the routine way – so after any crash, you may discover that ScanDisk takes over and performs its standard tests. However, even if your machine never crashes, problems can still arise with the hard disk and these can be detected by ScanDisk which will also be able to provide a remedy.

There are two options for ScanDisk. A

Standard test checks files and folders for errors and takes only a few minutes to complete. A Thorough test extends on this by adding a scan of the hard disk's surface. Depending on the size of the disk this can take a considerable time – allow around an hour for a 10Gb drive.

Making progress

Although there is a progress bar to show that the operation is proceeding it does not give a good indication of how much longer you are likely to wait. As long as nothing is detected by the standard test you need only perform a Thorough test at fairly long (but regular intervals).

So, what might ScanDisk discover? The most common problem is clusters that have become 'lost' – in other words, they are not part of a file and they are not included in the free space waiting to be used. Often lost clusters will belong to temporary files but if you have lost a valuable file it may be that recovering lost clusters will give you access to portions of it.

When ScanDisk finds lost clusters it asks if you want to save them to inspect them. Unless you are trying to locate items you

know to be lost you can probably let ScanDisk delete them automatically. When it finds parts of the disk that are physically damaged ScanDisk can mark them as unusable. This reduces the storage capacity of the hard disk but means that what is available is no longer error prone.

All hard disks have some areas that are unusable because of surface faults when they were manufactured. An area of a disk may become unusable because of a physical shock to the machine – knocking it over, for example – but if you find more and more areas of the disk are becoming unusable each time you run ScanDisk then this is a pretty good indication that the drive is failing.

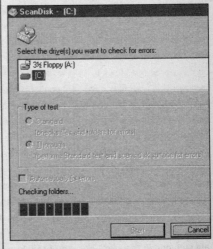

ScanDisk Results - (C:)
ScanDisk did not find any errors on this drive
10,006,696 KB total disk space
0 bytes in bad sectors
8,937,472 bytes in 1,031 folders
12,623,872 bytes in 341 hidden files
2,402,328,576 bytes in 23,488 user files
7,639,616 KB available on disk
8,192 bytes in each allocation unit
1,250,837 total allocation units on disk
954,952 available allocation units
Close

A screen informing you of the results after ScanDisk has been performed on your computer

The ScanDisk dialog box where you can decide which drive(s) you want to check out

Absolute Beginners:
keeping data safe

Most of us have valuable data stored on our computer. Here's our guide to keeping it safe

The first time many computer users stop to think about protecting their data is just after they have lost some precious data. Here we look at strategies for minimising the chance of data loss even in cases where your computer system crashes.

Computer equipment is generally reliable, so it can come as a bit of a shock to discover that your files have been corrupted or lost, but it can happen either as a result of human error or machine failure. Frighteningly, all it takes is a disruption of the electricity supply – a lightning strike, a spike or brown out on the power circuit or somebody pulling the plug out of its socket – to wipe out the file that you are

currently working on. The consequences when this happens can be catastrophic or merely a slight inconvenience, depending on the user and the nature of the work in question.

Imagine you are working on a word processor document, a spreadsheet, or a drawing when your computer suddenly stops working. You have already been working for two hours. How much effort are you going to lose? This is a trick question – the answer depends on your habits rather than any hard and fast rule. If your document has been given a name and has been saved at regular intervals then you will probably lose very little work. If you've not even

given the file a name and have worked without any of the forms of protection that Windows applications can offer then you may have lost all of it ... for good.

Making backups

When you save your work, you normally have the option of making a backup. The difference between a backup created in this way and an automatic timed backup is that when you save your work you also keep the previous version. This is a very useful safeguard if you are experimenting with documents or have a tendency to make mistakes. If you've messed up a document and have saved it after making these changes you can then open the backup rather than the main version.

The drawback of having backups is that they clutter up your filing system. It's because of this that most modern applications don't create backups by default. It's up to you to make a point of setting this option if you want it to be active.

In Microsoft Word, you can do it in the same Save dialog box we discussed above, which is accessed from the Tools, Options menu as well as File, Save As, Options. In Excel you can only do it from the Save As dialog box and the change only applies on a file-by-file basis. This means that if you have decided backup is a good idea you'll need to set the option individually for every spreadsheet you wish it to apply for.

Name and save

Here are three steps to help you avoid data loss –
1) When you create a new document you should give it a name. This makes it much more secure both in the event of machine failure and when it comes to human error. If you're prompted to save Document 4 you may close it without saving, and imagine how annoyed you will be when you realise that it was the new report you've spent three hours creating from scratch.
2) Get into the habit of saving at frequent intervals. Use Ctrl-S if you work mainly with the keyboard or click the disk icon in an application's main toolbar.
3) Avoid ALT-F4 and the Close box as a method of closing down your applications. Pressing ALT-F4 has the same effect as clicking the close box at the far right of an application's title bar.

These methods have their problems: they're universal, too quick to do and impossible to undo. If you're working on more than one application it's better to exit from each using its own file menu, this avoids the situation of thinking the current window contains a spreadsheet you don't want when in fact it has an important letter in it that you do.

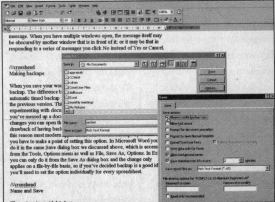

AutoRecover in Microsoft Word

AutoRecover is a feature that makes Microsoft Word a particularly safe environment to work in. When the AutoRecover feature is turned on, there is a good chance that data loss through external disasters, such as power loss, is kept to a minimum due to your file being automatically saved at regular and frequent intervals.

To make sure that you have the benefit of this facility you need to open Word's Save Options dialog box. Use either the Word command Tools, Options and click on the Save tab or click on the Options button in the Save As dialog. In this dialog ensure that there is a tick against 'Save AutoRecover info every:' and enter a suitable value in the minutes box. If you have the value set at three minutes you'll rarely lose more than a couple of

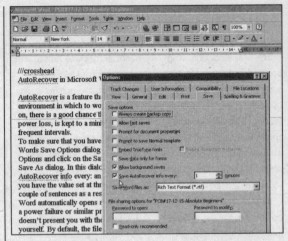

sentences as a result.

Word automatically opens any recovered documents when you restart after a power failure or similar problem. However, if for some reason Word doesn't present you with the recovered file in this way, you can open it yourself. By default, the file is located in the Temp folder in the Windows folder. When Word automatically opens a recovery file, the recovered file is deleted if you fail to save it, so do it immediately!

Other Office Software has similar facilities, referred to as timed backups in Corel Office and automatic time saves in Lotus SmartSuite.

AutoRecover and automatic timed backups only protect you in situations where the machine fails while you are working. They do not give protection in situations where you have worked on a document, made changes to it that you want to keep and then closed it without choosing to save. If you make this

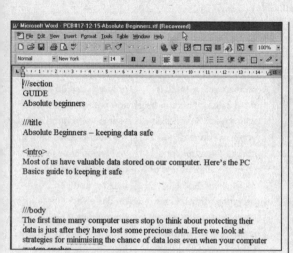

vital warning message. Also, the message itself may be obscured by another window, in front of it, or it may be that in responding quickly to a series of messages, you may click No instead of Yes or Cancel.

(The Undo command [Ctrl+Z] can be a lifesaver if you notice you have done something stupid and want to roll back one or more steps).

type of blunder then there is no easy way of recovering your work. This is because the temporary files kept by the application are deleted whenever you save or close a document.

You might imagine that you could never make such an error – after all, why would you ever ignore the type of message that applications normally present? The answer is that often when you're working on multiple tasks, you may discover that you have

too many windows open and start closing most of them down. In such cases it's all too easy to miss a

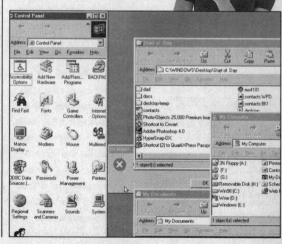

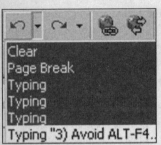

Ctrl-Z is the shortcut for Edit, Undo in Windows applications

Backup when prompted

Some applications are more backup conscious than others and usually with good reason. A prompt is produced at regular intervals by the personal finance manager, Quicken. The software manufacturers know that if you rely on your accounting software for day-to-day financial management, you will be lost if your computer lets you down. Take the advice and backup using a floppy disk whenever you are advised to do so.

If you are tempted to undo many steps, you would be better reverting to a previous version of the file!

Undo

Windows programs typically have an Undo feature (and a corresponding Redo in most cases). This can be a lifesaver if you notice you have done something stupid and want to roll back one or more steps. Some programs only let you Undo one action, some support a set number of Undo, while others allow you to choose the number to permit. When you start to use a new application discover its Undo limit and don't make the mistake of assuming it is infinite.

Backup?

When you select 'All selected files' you are opting for a Full backup. This is obviously what is needed the first time you backup your files but next time round you have a clear choice between Full and Incremental, where you simply backup the files that are new or have changed since the last backup. As the backup program can do this for you automatically it seems like a good option – an incremental backup will typically be very quick compared to a full backup and can often be done to a single floppy disk.

So why not choose incremental backup every time? Well consider what happens when you actually need the backup. When you have a Full backup to hand you can simply pop it into the drive and use the Restore backed up files command from the Microsoft Backup dialog. If you have been in the habit of doing Incremental backups, you still need the original Full backup plus all the subsequent Incremental ones.

The best strategy is to take a Full backup at

regular intervals. For example, if you back up daily, then you should do a Full backup once a week with Incremental backups on the other days. If you're using Zip diskettes for Full backup and floppy disks for the incremental ones label them clearly.

Having chosen your scheme, remember it's not enough to have a single set of backup disks, you need at least two sets and traditional wisdom dictates three. So the second time you do a full backup, DON'T use the Zip disk that already has the backed up data on it, use a new one. Only when you have a second complete backup can you re-use the first set and for extra insurance, use three.

More backup options

The Backup Wizard gives you two more options to consider and again you are trading safety against time and disk space. If you ask the computer to Compare and Verify the data the backup procedure will be much slower but any problems

will be discovered and can be corrected. If you're using an older backup device such as a streaming tape drive then it's wise to tick this option. When using a reliable device such as a Zip disk you should be OK, but you can always tick the option to be cautious.

When you opt to Compress the data you save disk space but also the operation is slower and risk of problems are increased. It's more difficult to restore Compressed files if the data is infected.

When you've made the choices, name the backup job for reference.

Other types of backup

1 CD Recordable discs can be written to only once.

2 CD ReWritable discs can be erased and reused.

3 A removable disk drive with 100Mb per diskette.

4 A higher capacity version of a Zip drive holding 1 or 2Gb per diskette.

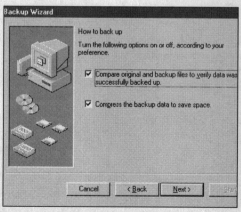

The two options available to you in Backup Wizard

The whole disk

We've looked at strategies for protecting individual files, but if you are using your computer for business purposes or for school or college work this probably isn't going to be enough. Think about what would happen if your entire hard disk was to be wiped – and while this is not an everyday occurrence it can and does happen. Does the thought make you slightly uneasy or does it make your blood run cold? If it's the latter then you need to devise a backup strategy NOW.

The software for backup is part of Windows 98 but the first problem to solve is what backup medium to use. There are several choices and the decision needs to be based on how much you need to back up and how frequently. Remember you don't need to back up everything on your computer. If the worst happens and you lose the contents of your disk you'll

have to reinstall Windows and the applications programs you use, so it's just the data files (which may only amount to a few megabytes) that you need to backup.

The Options

The cheapest backup option is floppy disks, but it's the most cumbersome solution and really only works well if you have only a handful of documents and data files. If you have no other backup device, use floppy disks to keep a copy of items such as your address

book and other personal information manager files, any accounts data you keep on computer and word processor documents that have current importance. But once the number of floppies you use creeps up to ten or more, consider an alternative that makes the procedure easier.

A Zip disk is a good device for selective backups, it stores 100Mb per diskette meaning most users can copy all their data onto a single Zip. A Jaz drive is a similar device but with higher

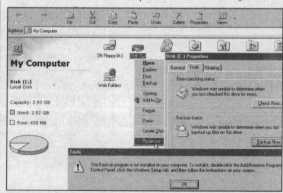

Once Microsoft Backup is installed by pressing Backup Now, it will initiate a simple procedure to create a backup job. This gives your computer the information needed to backup your precious files.

capacity, 1 or even 2Gb. Writing data out to writeable CD-ROMs is another option, but only really makes sense if you have other reasons to create CD-ROMs.

Another alternative is a removable hard drive – a good choice if you want to keep copies of programs as well as data, but backing up an entire hard disk takes a substantial amount of time.

Let's assume you've solved this problem and worked out where to keep your backups and have installed the relevant hardware. The software aspect is then very straightforward, though it may require you to install a program from the Windows CD-ROM.

Open My Computer, then, right-click the icon for your hard disc, Drive C: and select Properties. Go to the Tools section of the Properties dialog box and click the Backup Now button. If you've already used Microsoft Backup, when you open the Tools section, the Backup status section will show you when you last used it. If you then see this message follow its instructions and install the software.

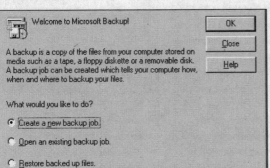

Click on Create a new backup job and click OK. The options to open an existing backup job and to restore backed up files can also be found at this point in the backup procedure

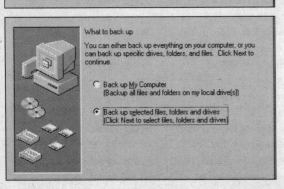

At the next step you can choose to back up all the files that are part of My Computer (in other words, the whole of Drive C: and any other local hard drives)

Absolute Beginners:
WordPad

Now we take a look at WordPad, the word processor that Windows automatically installs in the Accessories folder, and we compare it with the even more basic Notepad utility

Using Notepad

Windows Notepad is an ASCII text editor, a no-frills utility for working with plain text in the most basic of ways. As ever, the best way to discover what you can do with it is to try it out.

The file Test of WordPad1 differs in one significant way from the original Test of WordPad. In order to convert a document from WordPad to Notepad, it has to be saved in .txt format. If you try to open a .doc version, you will find a bewildering screen full of unfamiliar characters but with fragments of readable text interspersed.

By converting the file into ASCII text, something that has to be done using File, Save As in WordPad, you remove the

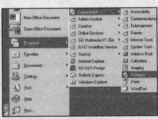

Open NotePad from the Start menu

unwanted garbage and see only the meaningful text content.

Even when you open a text-only file, what you see is a single line at the top of the screen. This is because NotePad doesn't automatically used word wrap. Instead you have to specify this option in the edit menu.

The edit menu has the Cut, Copy and Paste operations we met last month together with their keyboard shortcuts. There is also an Undo command but this quite a bit less useful that its counterpart in WordPad in that it only undoes the very last operation.

Compared to WordPad's menu, Notepad's is very sparse – and there are no icons, just words. It has File with the commands New, Open, Save and Save As – but, as we have already discovered, it only has one file format (.txt) for its Save operations.

The File menu also has two commands – Page Setup and Print for producing paper output. The Edit menu has the operations we've already discussed and also includes a command Set Font which can be used to change the Font from its default – a font called Fixedsys – to an alternative. The limitation with this is that the change applies to the entire document and not just to selected parts of it.

The third menu item is Search which opens a Find dialog. Notice that Notepad lacks the Replace facility that makes the find operation so powerful in WordPad.

Why Notepad?

So, why use Notepad at all, given that WordPad appears to offer so much more and is also available in the Accessories group? The answer is, because it is so simple!

It saves its file in plain ASCII text and can therefore be useful in situations where you cannot assume a computer user has any sophisticated facilities. Notepad is still sometimes used for the Read Me files to give otherwise undocumented information about software you install on your computer and it is worth knowing how to read files using it even if you don't want to create files this way.

Text effects

The main difference between Notepad's text-only files and the ones that can be created by WordPad is formatting – ways of embellishing text to make it more distinctive. Notice how WordPad, and other word processors you may use, has a Format menu. It also has a Format Bar and this provides an easier way of applying text effects and this can be turned on and off as an option in the View menu.

When you enter some text into WordPad without any regard to formatting, it would have used the default Font at its default point size. When the Format Bar is open, look at what is entered in the Font box and in the Font Size box. For example, the font used might be Times New Roman and the size might be 12 – but you may see different values in either box. The larger the value in the size box the larger the text on the printed page – and, in the case of WordPad, also on the screen. This is because WordPad has none of the zoom options which you find in other word processors which enlarge your view of the text on the screen display.

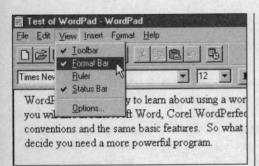

If the Format Bar is not already open, use the View menu and click Format Bar to place a tick beside it

Getting back to WordPad

To get back to a WordPad document, you can open WordPad using the Accessories group found in the Programs section Start menu. If, however, you have saved a file worked on previously, then you also might be able to use a shortcut to reopen the application using the Documents section of the start menu.

Click on the Start button to open the Start menu, highlight Documents and click on the name of the document you would like to open from the list that appears. This will open the document and the application most appropriate to

working with it.

However, if you have Microsoft Word on your machine, then this application will open in preference to WordPad.

Another method of launching both document and program is to double -click on its icon in its folder. If you saved it in the My Documents folder on the desktop then this is almost as quick an option as using the Start menu.

Finally, if none of these methods will open WordPad as well as the file created using it, then you will have to start WordPad first and then use its own File, Open command – or its Open icon – in order to work on any existing document.

Alignment

Let's take a look at alignment in WordPad now. Along the format bar there are three buttons that control line alignment. This is sometimes also referred to as 'justification'.

Notice how Align Left is automatically pushed in? The title line would look better if it was centred. To do this place the cursor anywhere within the line and left-click the Centre button.

You might also like to see what happens when you place the cursor within the longer paragraph and press the Centre button. The Right button is less frequently needed. Use it if you like to right align the date in a letter.

In a report or similar document it is sometimes the convention to conclude with your name and the date, or the place and date of the document's origination. When you want to insert a date or a time into a WordPad document you don't need to consult a calendar – as long as your computer clock is set correctly, that is.

Assuming this is the case, having typed in either your name or a place name on one line, press Enter (to force a carriage return) and left-

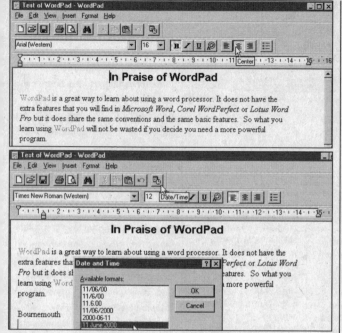

Clicking on the centre button aligns the chosen text to the middle

The date and time can easily be applied to the document

click the Date/Time button in the Toolbar. This opens the Date and Time dialog and you can select the format in which you would like the date (or time) to be displayed. Once this date is in the document, it is fixed – it will not update when you re-open the document for editing.

When you have text items on separate lines as here, each is treated as a new paragraph. In order to right justify both lines in a single operation, you need to select them both and then click on the Align Right button.

Before you try experimenting with line alignment, check the Word Wrap options in the View menu and ensure that Wrap to Ruler is set rather than Wrap to Window.

It could also be extremely helpful to you to display the ruler itself. Again this can be done using the View menu.

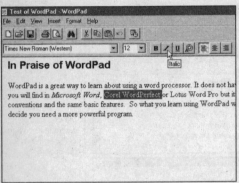

To make the names of the proprietary word processors stand ou,t select each in turn and apply italic style

Size of the display

To zoom in or out while using WordPad, go to the Desktop and right-click on an empty area. In the pop-up menu, Select Properties and click on the Settings tab. Drag the slider on the bottom left (drag it left to enlarge the screen display and right to shrink it). You may need to restore it to the original setting for other programs as some will only work at specific screen displays. 12 point type is a very suitable size for printing, it's large enough to read without strain without being too "big". Times New Roman is a good font for large passages of text because the embellishments at the end of individual letters lead the eye on.

To put all the text already in this document into 12 point Times New Roman, use the Select All command. This is on the Edit menu, but like all frequently used Windows commands there is a keyboard short cut which is well worth knowing about – Ctrl-A. With a passage of text as short as this you could also use the mouse to select all of it if you prefer using the mouse to the keyboard.

If you need to alter the font used, click the arrow at the left of the Font box and scroll down the list to find Times New Roman. Alternatively with the list open type "Ti" to jump to the correct part of the list. You may find many variants on Times New Roman in which case Times New Roman (Western) is the appropriate choice. There are two ways to alter the size of the text. You can either type 12 into the box or select it from the drop-down list.

While Notepad only allows you to use a single font throughout a document, you can use as many as you want to in WordPad. It is however considered good practice only to use a small number of font types and to use a sans serif font such as Arial for titles and headings. Headings normally use a larger point

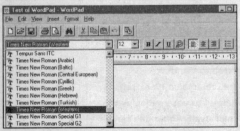

You can choose which font you prefer in the Font box

Tab stops

There is one more feature in the Format menu that we have not yet considered and that is Tabs. If you want to set a tab stop at a specific point, or if you want to clear an existing tab or all of them, then the command Format, Tabs opens a dialog box that lets you do all these operations. However, when the ruler is on view you can also do this interactively. Clicking at a point on the ruler sets a tab at that point in the current paragraph. If you want a tab

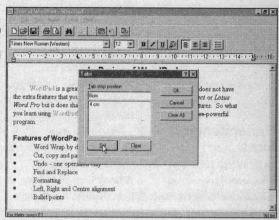

Use tabs to break up the document and give a professional look

to apply to the whole of a document set tabs at the very outset. Alternatively to include tab stops throughout an existing one use the Select All command first. You can remove tabs by dragging them off the ruler to the left or the right. WordPad has only one type of tab – a left tab, whilst more sophisticated word processors offer right, centre and decimal tabs.

---

size combined with bold to make them stand out.

To enter the heading shown here, move the cursor to the start of the document (or use Ctrl+Home, i.e. press the Home key while Ctrl is held down to jump there) and press the Enter key twice to create a space. Then move the cursor back to before the space. You can format the heading before or after typing it. If you prefer to do

it prior to typing select Arial from the Font dropdown list, 16 from the Size dropdown list and click on the Bold icon (just to the right of the Size dropdown list) so that it appears 'pressed in' and then type the heading text. If you prefer to format after typing type in the text in the font already in force – i.e. Times New Roman in 12-point – then select the newly-typed words and while it is highlighted, carry

out the same three operations.

Bold is just one of three Font styles that can be applied using the Format bar. The others are Italic and Underline. As well as applying formatting to a paragraph or a line of text you can also format a phrase or single word or even one or more letters with a word. The easiest way to do this is after entering the text, by selecting the text you want to modify using the mouse (or equivalent keyboard methods as discussed in the previous article) and then selecting the attribute.

Understanding fonts

As far as standard typography is concerned there are two basic types of font – serif and 'sans' serif. Serifs are the curly embellishments at the end of letters and 'sans' means without and so a sans serif font is plain and clean compared to a serif one. Times Roman is the archetypal serif font and Arial is the most commonly used sans serif font. Comparing individual letters in these two fonts at a large point size reveals the salient differences between them.

As you add more software to your computer you will discover that the list of fonts you have available grows and grows and it becomes more and more difficult to categorise them

into 'serif' and 'sans serif'.

The word 'font' is sometimes used to mean a typeface – Times New Roman, Arial, Courier and so on. More properly a combination of typeface, point size and style attributes – so 12 point Ariel and 14 point Arial are different fonts and adding bold produces further fonts.

Point size – a point is 1/72 of an inch. This suggests that in 8 point type a letter could measure 1/9 of an inch and in 12 point type 1/6 of an inch. This is too simplistic as there is a lot of variance

according to which letter you measure and whether you consider upper case or lower case letters and there is also variance between fonts. It is however a useful yardstick for comparisons within a specific font.

Colour

An alternative way to add emphasis is to use colour and WordPad makes this particularly easy by having a Colour button just next to those for bold, italic and underline. If you select some text and then click on this button, you are given 16

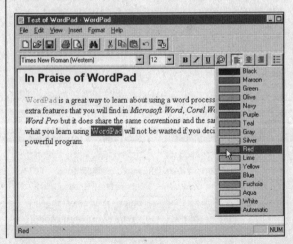

colours to choose from – and their names are listed to make repeating the choice easier. To try it out make occurrences of WordPad appear in Red.

Bullet points

The final button in the formatting toolbar adds bullet points. Again, this is something that you often want to apply to a series of single-line paragraphs, as in this example. Select all the lines (paragraphs) you want to embellish in this way and then simply click on the bullets icon.

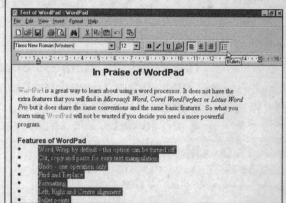

Right-click menu

A PC mouse has two buttons and over recent generations of software the right button has gathered more functions. Click the right mouse button in Notepad and nothing happens, but in WordPad (and more sophisticated word processors) you will see a list of context-sensitive tasks.

If you have a word or phrase selected when you right-click, the menu includes Cut, Copy and Paste. The Font dialog is available from the right-click menu. This gathers together all the options we discussed earlier, including colour and size. The only new option it offers is Strikeout, placing a line through selected text.

The Bullet Style option on the right-click menu does nothing more than the icon in the Format Bar, but the Paragraph dialog has an extra feature. It lets you set an indentation for the first line of a paragraph.

This dialog box, like the Font dialog, can also be opened via the Format command in the main Toolbar at the top of the screen.

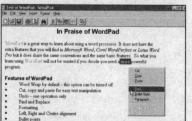

Right-click on the mouse to bring up a pop-up menu

Choose the style you prefer from a variety of fonts

Absolute Beginners:
the address book

The Windows Address Book turns up everywhere – and that is why it is so important to start using it and keeping it up to date. We show you how to update, add, organise and edit all your contacts

Getting to know the Address Book

When you open an Address Book what you'll see is a list with just a few details – Name, email Address and Phone numbers. This is just part of the information stored in the address book. For more information about one of the people in the list you'll need to view their ¡Properties¡. As ever with a Windows application their are many ways of doing this. If you just need to check an address then hovering the cursor over a name turns it blue and displays a yellow tip box that shows all the details you have stored on that person. The same tip box appears if you click once with the left mouse button on a name to highlight the entry. If you do this, notice that it initially appears against a blue background, which turns to grey if you switch back to the address book after moving to another application.

The advantage of selecting an entry in this way is that as well as viewing the information you can also copy it into you word processor, for example, simply by using the command Edit, Copy (or its shortcut Ctrl+C) and then using Edit, Paste (Ctrl+V) in the application where you require the information.

Update your contacts

When you want to change or add to the information you have about a contact, then you need to open the Properties dialog. There are many ways to do this, the simplest of which is to double-click on a name in the list. If the name is already highlighted then just press Enter to open it or click on the Properties button in the address book's main toolbar. If you like using the right mouse button to access pop-up menus, the one in this situation gives an alternative to using the toolbar. Finally you can access Properties from the File menu and using the keyboard shortcut of Alt+Enter.

You will often find it helpful to have your address book open at the same time as another program – your word processor, spreadsheet or Outlook Express for example. You may well have three or more applications on the go at once and want to switch between them. One way is to use the Taskbar – when an application is minimised or is not the active window then clicking on its name in the Taskbar makes it active and brings it to the front. Another is to press Alt+Tab. This cycles around the available applications, going first to the one that was most recently used.

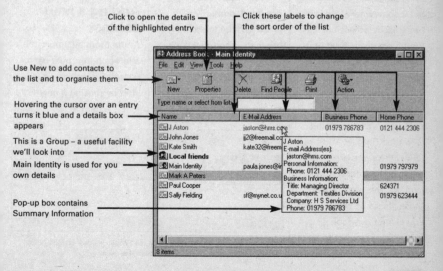

Click to open the details of the highlighted entry

Click these labels to change the sort order of the list

Use New to add contacts to the list and to organise them

Hovering the cursor over an entry turns it blue and a details box appears

This is a Group – a useful facility we'll look into

Main Identity is used for you own details

Pop-up box contains Summary Information

You might not think of the Address Book as falling into the Windows Accessories Group, as you might be more used to encountering it in other places such as Outlook Express or Microsoft Works. However, it can be found by clicking on the Start button, clicking on Program, then on Accessories and finally on Address Book.

If you don't currently use applications that force you to keep your address book up to date then you need to put it somewhere that is more easily accessible. Last month we discovered how to place the Calculator icon on the Desktop and add it to the group of Quick Launch icons simply by dragging it while holding down the Ctrl key. You can follow the same procedure to place the Address Book icon in either (or both) of these places as well, so that you cannot overlook it.

You might expect to be able to open the Windows Address Book every time you click on an address book icon in a Windows application. You can from many of them – Microsoft Works 2000 relies on it for example, and if you use Corel WordPerfect then it is one of the choices you are presented with.

If you use Microsoft Office, however, there is no straightforward route to the Windows Address book – well not as yet. The reason for this ludicrous situation is that the Windows Address Book was designed, primarily with email and the Internet in mind, to support Outlook Express. The programming team who developed it seemed to be unaware that Microsoft Office already had a Personal Address Book that could be shared between Word, Access and Outlook. Undoubtedly in the not too far distant future, Microsoft will come up with a fix for the problem. Until then we include details of how to use data from the Windows Address Book in Microsoft Word, in the article iMaking An Impact with Mail Mergeî, and this approach allows the data to be used in other office applications as well.

Adding a new contact

At the moment, your address book could be completely empty, so lets start by making a new entry. Although it is

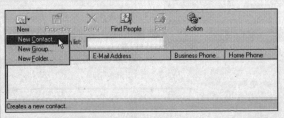

An empty address book – notice that the Properties box and the delete button are greyed out as they cannot yet be used.

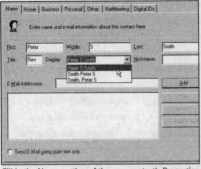

Fill in the Name section of the new contact's Properties

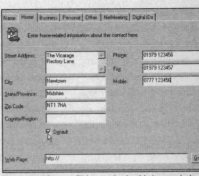

The second form to fill in – notice its title bar reminds you whose details to type

possible to remove entries very easily, it is rather a waste of time making dummy entries just to delete them – so think of a personal friend and type in his or her name and other details. Remember it's your address book, so record everything that you might possibly want. The entry can always be edited later if you do not have all the information to hand.

There are several ways to start. Clicking the New button in the toolbar is the most obvious, but if you prefer the keyboard to using the mouse use the shortcut Ctrl+N.
Notice that the Properties

dialog only has seven sections – all of them forms. The Summary Page will only be added once you have entered at least a name and click OK.

The first section of the new contact's Properties is Name. Notice that there are three name boxes First, Middle and Last and that you press the Tab key to move between them – if you press Enter at any stage the Address Book will think you have completed the record! If you want to jump to a box without using the Tab key you can press the Alt key down and type in the letter for the box, e.g. L for last but D

for Middle – you need to look carefully at the box labels to see which letter is underlined.

Notice that the Display field is automatically completed as you type into these boxes. If you press the down arrow next to it you have three choices about the name to be displayed in the address book. You can also edit the contents of this box. In this case we want it to include the person's title and not to include his middle initial. Having made any such changes you require click the Home tab.

On moving to the Home section, notice that the title

bar has changed – it now contains the display name you have used for this contact. The next thing to notice is that the field names are American rather than English. This does not affect their usefulness but you do need to use them in a consistent way. Use City for the main place in the address and State/Province for county or conurbation. These days by far the most important item is the Postcode and this goes into the Zip Code field.

It is worth typing in full phone numbers, STD code included. This will make copying the information to documents that require complete details easier and is also useful future-proofing. Even if you don't use the program's dialling capabilities now, you might at some time in the future – and there's no harm in dialling a redundant code.

In the case of a personal friend you probably want the Home address to be the Default – the one that is offered automatically – so tick this Default box.

That's probably all the information you want about many of your acquaintances but in the case of your closest friends you may find the

Organising your contacts

An address list can become very long! You can, however, manage it in two distinct ways – Folders and Groups. The idea of Folders will already be familiar to you from working with files and folders. You can use Folders in order to organise your contacts into categories. It might be useful, for example, to reduce the number of names on view by putting infrequent contacts into a folder.

Groups have a functional role and a contact can be a member of more than one group – so if you use groups such as Family, Friends and Business a single contact could be a member of all three. This Address Book has an existing group of Local Friends – created for the purpose of a mailmerge operation in which they were all being invited to an event.

Create a group using the New button and selecting New Group. You then type in a Name for the Group. There's also a Group Details form, which is useful if it's a club

with an address or a Web page. From the former Group page, clicking Select Member opens a scrolling window listing all your contacts on the left. Highlight a name and click the Select button to copy the record to the list on the right. You can also add new contacts to the Address Book from this window and thinking about Groups is a good way to ensure that you add all your contacts to your Windows Address Book.

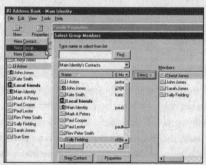

Use Groups to organise your contacts.

Windows Address Book a useful place to put dates and family. There's a field for the name of the person's spouse, then you can enter details of several children by clicking Add as often as required and entering the name in place of new child. The Gender field is for the contact and is initially Unspecified – the drop-down list contains Male and Female so you don't have to type. The Birthday and Anniversary fields are initially set to today's data and are greyed out. Click in the box to tick it if you want to use this field. There's a drop-down calendar available, but it's quicker to type in the year rather than alter it interactively!

Email addresses

Up until now we have overlooked the email address section on the name page, but as the Windows Address Book is central to Outlook

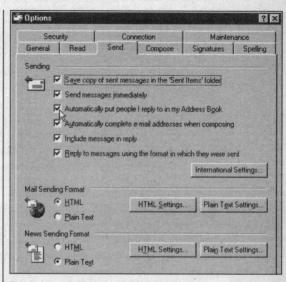

Ensure the email address is correctly formed

Express, the email program you are most likely to be using, it is certainly worth knowing how to add email addresses to it.

The most obvious way is to type into the Email Addresses box on the Name page of the Properties dialog for your friends and acquaintances. If you've just written an email and Outlook cannot find the name you have used, you will see this message and can click the New Contact box to enter it. (If you are sure you have entered the name, click Show More Names to see the full list in your Address Book.)

When entering an email address type it all in lower case and be scrupulous about punctuation marks – there's an underscore in this address but sometimes both names are run together, sometimes there's a full

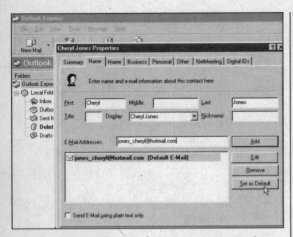

are likely to have more than one email address – one for home, another for work and so on.

Having typed in the first email address click the Add button. This transfers the information to the list box underneath the email addresses box and you can enter the next address. When you enter the first email address it is automatically treated as the Default, but you can make any address the one used for preference by the Default button.

When using Outlook

stop or a hyphen. There is always an @ between the name and the service used and there's always a full stop before the final element – e.g. .com for an international service; co.uk for a UK-specific or .es for a Spanish one.

Some of your contacts

A Business Contact

When you enter a Business contact you are faced with a rather more extensive form. Again, just enter the details you are interested in. Notice that as the Windows Address Book has been designed with the Internet in mind there is a Web Page box (just as there is on the Home form). If you have an Internet connection, enter a web page and use the Go button to see the link in action – but remember if you pay for phone connection time, do this at a convenient moment.

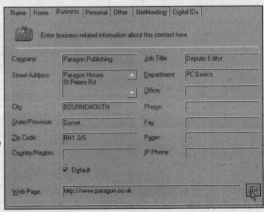

A comprehensive list of contact details

Express, you can save yourself time and trouble by automatically recording the email address of anyone you reply to – i.e. on receiving a message from a new contact you use the Reply button to send a response. Ensure that there is a tick against 'Automatically put people I reply to in my Address Book' in the Send section of the Options dialog accessed via Tools, Options.

If you don't want to use Reply but do want the address from an incoming message, right-click on it in your inbox and select Add to Address Book – you can do the same with messages in your Sent box.

Ensure the email address is correctly formed

Existing record

All you have to do to edit an existing record is to open the contact's Properties. You can then add extra information or delete or amend details already there.

Why use nicknames?

You'll notice there's a box for a Nickname in the Name section of Properties. This may seem a little strange. In fact it can be quite helpful as a shortcut. Say you have lots of contacts in your list whose names start the same way – Joe, Joanne, John Hunt, John Smith or John Talisker - and one you frequently email, John Taylor, which comes last in this list alphabetically, because of the way Outlook Express uses autocomplete to match names, you have to type in almost all this name before the correct name is provided. Allocating a nickname that provides a unique string for the contact, JT for example, saves a lot of typing and avoids sending messages to the wrong person by accepting the wrong default match. When choosing a nickname for convenience, bear in mind the need for a short name (ideally two characters) that is only going to result in the required record being matched. If you use such a nickname the recipient won't even know you've abbreviated the name as they will see the display name it is associated with. You can, however, use the contents of the Nickname field as the display name – when you make an entry in the Nickname field it is added to the list of Display options.

Absolute Beginners:
windows secrets

Microsoft have done its best to explain the basics of the latest Windows operating system, but there are still plenty of handy little tools and tricks that you haven't been told about. We reveal all

Windows 95 was complicated enough, but Windows 98 is a far more complex beast. There's so much crammed into it that even if you know numerous tips and tricks relating to the operating system, the chances are you've hardly scratched the surface.

However, here at PC Home we pride ourselves on knowing all there is to know about Windows 98. And, being generous souls, we thought we'd share some of that knowledge with you. So hold on tight and get ready as we reveal the best Windows 98 secrets that can help make using your PC just that little bit easier...

I've only got 95!

Oddly enough if you're still running Windows 95 you'll probably be able to get a fair bit of use out of a lot of these Windows 98 secrets. How's that possible? Well a lot of the changes introduced with Windows 98 come about thanks to Internet Explorer 4 (now up to version 5). If you install Internet Explorer

4 or higher on a Windows 95 machine you automatically get a lot of the advantages that Windows 98 offers.

Global viewing

Would you like to use the same View options, such as Details and Arrange Icons by Date, for all open folder windows? The inability to set these options globally was one of the shortcomings of Windows 95; but in Windows 98 you can set your system's default viewing options from any open folder window.

Open any folder window (such as My Computer) and use the View menu to set the viewing options you'd like for every folder. Next, select View/Folder Options and, in the resulting dialog box, click the View tab. Click the Like Current Folder button, click Yes to confirm, then OK. From now on, every folder window will open with these same View options already set.

Make all your windows use the same view

Thumbnail viewing

Windows 98 gives you two ways of viewing picture files and Web pages as thumbnails. This is helpful if you want to see what a file is without having to open it. The first and simplest way is to open the folder that has the files and select the View/as Web Page menu option. Double click the window's title bar so the window fills the screen. If you now select a picture or Web page a preview thumbnail will be displayed in the left part of the window along with a few details about it, very handy.

Icon thumbnails

If you want something a little more substantial you can get Windows to display all the files in a folder as little thumbnails of themselves. A word of warning though, on slower machines this can drastically slow down folder listings.

Select the folder in which you want to display thumbnails, right click it and select Properties. Near the bottom of the properties window select the Enable thumbnail view tick box.

Click OK and open the folder, now all you need to do is select the View/Thumbnails option. Any picture files or Web pages will have little thumbnails made for them instead of icons. Just select View/List to revert back to how things were.

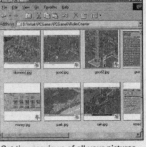

Get tiny previews of all your pictures

Hide the channel bar

Internet Explorer 4 and Windows 98 altered the way your desktop works with the addition of the active desktop. This makes it possible to actually have Web pages displayed as part of the desktop. It sounds clever, and it is. The problem is, however, that active desktop seems to make all but the fastest machines crawl along.

To turn off active desktop right click a blank area of the desktop and select Active desktop. Make sure View as Web page doesn't have a check

The documents folder

Some of you may not appreciate the subtleties of the new My Documents icon that has appeared on the Windows 98 Desktop. It is in fact a specially disguised shortcut, perform a right-click on it and all will be revealed.

Your first reaction may be to remove the little blighter with the Remove from Desktop option, but a quick trip to the Properties menu opens another window. By using the Browse button you can then target the My Documents icon to point to any folder you like on your computer. This means you can have a constant single shortcut to your regular work folder.

But what if you have deleted the My Documents icon only now to discover just how useful it can be? A simple right click on the Desktop, select New and My Documents Folder on Desktop and, hey presto, the icon reappears.

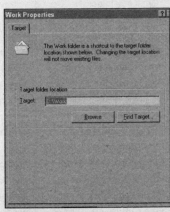

Point the My Documents icon to wherever you want it to go

mark beside it. A nice knock on effect of this is that it will also remove that pesky channel bar you probably never use.

Start where you want

Are you getting sick of visiting the MSN homepage every time you start Internet Explorer? Well it's actually possible to set any page you like as the default start page or even just start on a blank page.

This involves the Internet Options control panel so double-click My Computer, then Control Panel and the Internet Options icon. The top part of the General tab is called Home page in the text box you can enter the Web site you want to start with, or click the Blank button to start with no page at all. To makes things simpler browse to the page you want to start with, get to this window and click the Use Current button.

Better looks

There are a few little tricks you can try to alter how Windows looks and works. You may have noticed that whenever you open windows, menus or lists there is a funny little animation. Annoying eh? You can stop these by right clicking on a blank area of the desktop and selecting Properties. Switch to the Effects tab and make sure the tick box next to 'Animate windows, menus and lists' is clear.

In the same area you

Sort your Start menu

Need to rearrange one of your Start menu items? In Windows 95, you needed to do this type of rearranging in the Start menu window; now all it takes is a simple click and drag.

Select Start and navigate your way to the folder or item you want to move. Left mouse click the item and, while holding the left mouse, button navigate your way back or forward through the Start menu to this item's new home. (Just hold the mouse pointer over any menu you'd like to expand, as usual.) When you see a black, horizontal line in this space, let go and the item will appear in its new location.

Leave a shortcut to your favourite program on the desktop by dragging programs from the Start menu to your desktop using the same technique.

You can now drag and drop menu items in the Start menu

can improve the look of Windows icons by ticking Show icons using all possible colours.

You can also make Windows fonts look better, particularly larger fonts used in Web pages, headlines in documents and elsewhere by making sure the Smooth edges of screen fonts. tick box is checked. This will give any larger fonts smoother edges, with no jagged curves.

Finally there is an option which is more of a novelty rather than genuinely useful. If you check the tick box next to

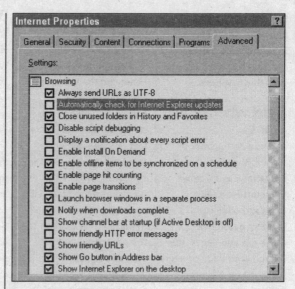

Stop Internet Explorer crashing and taking the rest of Windows with it

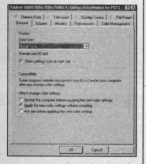

This adds a handy little monitor icon to your taskbar, with which you can switch through resolutions on the fly

Show windows contents while dragging when you move windows or resize them the window will stay solid instead of just showing the box outline. Avoid this if you have a slower machine (a Pentium 200MHz or less), as it can slow things down.

Quick display change

Do you need to change the size or resolution of your desktop on a regular basis? Normally you have to right click on a blank area of the desktop, select Properties and adjust the desktop size through the Display control panel.

However, there is a way of putting a little monitor icon in your taskbar that lets you quickly switch between desktop sizes. Right click a blank area of the desktop and select Properties. Switch to the

Settings tab and click the Advanced button. Make sure the Show settings icon on task bar box is ticked and click OK. This will put a monitor icon in the task bar, click on this and you get a list of different desktop sizes you can run. This allows you to switch between them on the fly, which can come in very handy.

Fewer crashes

If you browse the Web frequently you may notice that when Internet Explorer crashes it seems to take the whole of Windows with it, causing you to have to restart. Here's a handy little hint that can stop this happening.

Double click My Computer, then Control Panel and the Internet Options icon. Switch to the Advanced tab and carefully scan down the list of options. You should see one called Launch browser windows in a separate process make sure the tick box next to this is checked. Click OK to set the change.

Originally Internet Explorer was run through Windows Explorer. So when Internet Explorer crashed so did Windows Explorer. By changing this setting Internet Explorer will run as a separate program.

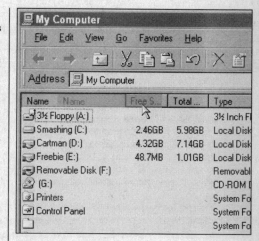

Move and resize these columns how you want them

Move and resize columns

If you regularly use the Detail view in Windows Explorer or in normal folder windows you might be glad to know you can alter how the detail columns are positioned and sized.

For example, if you double-click My Computer and select the View/Details menu option you'll see the four details columns appear in the window. If you now left click and hold the top of one of the columns and drag it to the left or right you can change the order that the columns appear.

In a similar way you can give one column more room or reduce the size of it. A very thin indented line divides each column, left click and hold this line and drag it to the left or right. This resizes the columns bordering the line, letting you alter the size.

It is also possible to resize a column so it disappears. It's still there, just very thin. To get it back, just do the same again but make sure you drag to the right of the line.

Cache more

Another Web related tip now. Double click My Computer, then Control Panel and the Internet Options icon. Under the initial General tab spot there's an area in the middle titled Temporary Internet files. Click the Settings button.

Using the slider bar you can allocate more hard drive space to storing cached Internet files. So what does that do? As you browse Web pages Internet Explorer stores all those little graphics and pages on your hard drive. If you then revisit the site and Internet Explorer finds that nothing has changed, instead of downloading all of the graphics again it just loads them from your hard drive, so speeding up the whole process. To make sure you don't fill up your Web cache, increase the size to around 200Mb, (provided your hard drive is a decent size of course).

Alter the cache settings to store more Web sites and graphics on your hard drive

Toolbars

This is something that has been mentioned in past issues of PC Home, but toolbars always come in so handy we'll cover them in more detail here. Toolbars are perfect for leaving programs, files, folders and Web sites that you use regularly out on the desktop without interfering with other icons.

Many people have three toolbars, one for tools another for Web sites and one for accessing other computers in the office. It just makes things more convenient.

Normally your toolbar is hiding as part of the taskbar running along the bottom of the screen. If you haven't changed it before you should find it just to the right of the Start button. It should already have four little icons in there. If it isn't there, don't worry you'll find out how to make your own later.

1 Spot the so-called Quick Launch toolbar nestling down by the Start button, the first thing to note is the little raised bar, these handles let you move the toolbar around. So to give the Quick Launch toolbar more room, left click and hold the bar on the right and slide it to the right, this makes the taskbar smaller. You can tell when the bar can be grabbed as the cursor changes to left/right arrow.

2 Now let's start adding things to the Quick Launch toolbar. A simple drag and drop operation is all you need to do. Left click and hold and icon you like to add, drag it over to the Quick Launch toolbar and drop it. A mini icon will appear in the toolbar. Click it as you would double click the icon on your desktop. Do the same for folders, files and programs in the Start menu – just drag them over.

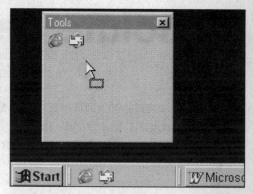

3 So maybe you don't want to keep the Quick Launch toolbar stuck down there as part of the main taskbar? Grab the left-hand vertical handle and drag it to an empty area of the desktop. When you release the mouse button the toolbar turns into a new window that you can move and resize as you would with any other window.

4 These floating toolbars, or palettes as they are sometimes called, have a number of extra options you may want to change. If you right click anywhere over a blank area of the toolbar you get a menu of options you can change, such as icon size, whether the icon name should be shown and whether the toolbar should float over any other windows or programs that are open.

5 If you drag this floating palette to the side of the desktop it turns back into a toolbar clinging to the side of the screen. If you want the toolbar on the side of the screen, but not taking up the width of the whole screen, drag the left edge over to the side of the screen where you want it to appear and then drag the other side to fit.

Absolute Beginners:
top tips

An army of writers have scoured the lands to bring you the most useful hints and tips to make working with your PC a little easier

Windows

1 Get quick access to your favourite files. Save yourself time by creating a shortcut to any document you regularly load. Simply hold down the right mouse button, drag the file onto your desktop and select Shortcut.

2 You can make Windows automatically minimise the applications you have it start up when it loads. In Windows 95 or NT, right click the icon, select Properties, click Shortcut and for the Run drop-down list box select Minimised.

3 For quicker access to your floppy drive, place a shortcut on the desktop. In Explorer, My Computer, or any folder window, right-click the A drive icon and drag it to the desktop. When you let go, select Create Shortcut(s) Here.

You can create shortcuts to any drive you like on your Desktop

4 Quicker startups. Want to get to work a little faster? You can prevent the applications in your StartUp folder from loading when Windows starts by holding down Shift as Windows loads.

5 If your old CD-ROM drive doesn't play audio CDs automatically, you can at least make it play them semi-automatically. Right click the desktop and select New...Shortcut. Enter the command line c:\windows\cdplayer.exe /play. Click Next, name the Shortcut and click

Finished. Now all you need do is pop in a CD and double click the new shortcut.

6 Want to have some fun with your mouse cursors? Select Start...Control Panel, double click Mouse and go to the Pointers page. Highlight the pointer you'd like to change, click Browse and double click a pointer you want to change to. Select Apply or OK to make your change stick.

7 In Explorer you can jump to any folder or file by typing the first few letters of its name very quickly. Don't type too slowly or Windows will jump to a file whose name begins with the second letter you type.

8 Want to get a printout from the File Manager or Explorer screen? Press .

Then open up Microsoft Paint or any other paint package, select Edit...Paste and print your screen.

9 Are you always pressing Caps Lock, Scroll Lock or Num Lock by mistake, only to discover your error later? You can get those keys to make a sound when you press them so you will never tap them by mistake again. Go to Control Panel, double click Accessibility Options, select Use ToggleKeys and click OK.

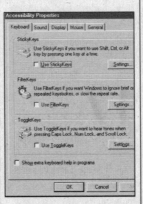

Use the accessibility control panel to make a chime when you press the Caps lock or Num lock keys

10 Switching an open folder to an Explorer view is an easy and efficient way to browse from folder to folder. To open an Explorer view, right click the icon in the upper left corner of the window and choose Explore.

11 You can use Notepad to create a time stamped log file – a handy tool for logging your voice mail or creating a to-do list. Simply type **.LOG** as the only text in the first line of a Notepad file. Then make your entries, save the file and close it. Next time you open the file, you'll see that Notepad has added a time and date stamp beneath each entry.

12 If you tend to work with windows that are taller than they are wide, move the Taskbar to the side of the screen. Click and hold and empty area of the Taskbar and drag it towards another edge of the Desktop, it will snap to the edge of the screen. Release the mouse button to fix it in place.

13 Make the Start menu more manageable by displaying small icons. Right click the Taskbar, select Properties and check Show small icons in the Start menu.

14 Move your most-used programs and menus out of the Programs menu and onto the Start menu. Windows 98 and IE 4 users can drag and drop folders and programs in the Start menu. Otherwise right click on the Start icon and select Explore.

15 For the fastest keyboard access to the Start menu items, rename your menu Shortcuts so that each starts with a unique letter. This allows you to just tap the start letter of the folder or program you want to select.

16 Find an attractive picture and turn it into wallpaper. Convert it into a .bmp file using a program such as PaintShop Pro and save it in c:\windows. Right click over the desktop, select Properties, click the Background tab and make your selection.

17 Add your most common destinations for files to the Send To menu. Create shortcuts to those folders in the Send To folder found in your c:/Windows folder. If you want to copy a file to one of these destinations just right

click on the file and select the Send To entry and the folder of choice.

18 Are Microsoft's default colours hard on your eyes? Right click the desktop, choose Properties, click the Appearance tab and pick something you like. Muted colours are easier to look at.

19 Don't like the on-screen font? Right click the desktop, choose Properties, click the Appearance tab, select something from the Item list and adjust the font and type size to your taste.

20 Position shortcuts and other desktop icons along the edge of the screen, where you can see them and get to them even when you have applications open.

21 Think 'My Computer' is a silly name? Change it as you would any other file name. Just click on it, press F2 and tap in the new name.

22 For quick access, limit shortcuts to high-priority documents on your desktop unless you are running a particularly high resolution desktop.

23 Reduce clutter by storing lower priority documents in a folder on the desktop.

Performance

24 Is your Windows system performing poorly? If you find your computer crashes when you try to run a good few programs your hard disk 'swap file' may not have enough room to do its thing. It needs free disk space to store information that your currently running programs need but cannot fit into your real memory. Try freeing up some drive space on your C: drive by getting rid of old unused files. Rid your system of old .tmp files. In Windows, use Find. Sort the files by date and then delete those without today's date.

25 If your system crashes when you open My Computer, Exchange, Control Panel or Recycle Bin, it could be because you have these three conditions: Your icon spacing is set to a large number or to 0. Your video resolution is set to 640x480 and you've placed your Taskbar along the right or left edge of the screen and made it larger than the default size. Increase your display size to overcome the problem, even if you have to reduce the number of colours used.

26 Reboot After a Crash. No matter what version of Windows you use, always reboot your system after an error crashes an application. If you don't Windows could become even more unstable and crash again, probably in the middle of an important project.

27 A bit of prevention, part 1. Regular disk maintenance helps keep your system stable. Check for disk errors at least once a month. With Windows 95, select Start...Programs... Accessories...System Tools...ScanDisk.

Use Scandisk to make sure your drives never have errors

28 A bit of prevention, part 2. You're more likely to lose files when your hard drive is fragmented and Windows simply runs slower, so you should defragment your drive at least once a month. With Windows 95 and 98, you'll find the Disk Defragmenter under Start...Programs...Accessories...System Tools.

29 Emergency start-ups. If you can't boot your hard drive, you'll be glad you have a start-up floppy

disk handy. To create one, from Control Panel double click Add/Remove Programs. Insert your disk, select the Startup Disk tab and click Create Disk. Just follow the instructions.

30 How hard is your CPU working? From the Start menu, select Programs...Accessories...System Tools...System Monitor. If System Monitor isn't there, you'll need to install it. Put your Windows disc in your CD-Rom drive. When the blue Windows window comes up, click Add/Remove Programs. Click the Windows Setup tab, double click Accessories, check System Monitor and click OK twice.

Data Security

31 Password-protecting Windows' screensaver will give you some protection from nosy colleagues. Right click your desktop, select Properties click the ScreenSaver tab and select a screensaver. Then check Password protected and click Change to enter a password, just don't forget it.

32 Conceal your entire past. To erase the Start menu's Documents list entirely, at least until you next create or save a file, right click an empty spot on the Taskbar, select Properties, click the Start Menu Programs tab, click Clear and then click OK.

33 Fine-tune your battery life. You can conserve battery power on a notebook PC by setting Windows to do a minimal amount of disk caching. Right click My Computer and select Properties. From the Performance tab, click File System. On the Hard Disk tab, make sure mobile or docking system is selected under Typical role of this machine.

34 For easy backups, keep all your data files in a single folder. To organise your data, put it in sub folders within that folder, by project or whatever other division makes sense to you. Windows 98 and IE4 users should take advantage of the My Documents folder on the desktop.

35 Once you're keeping your data in a single folder, tell your applications that is the default location to which they should save new files. How you do this varies from application to application and may take a bit of looking to figure it out. For instance, in Microsoft Word select Tools...Options, click the File Locations tab and modify the Documents option.

36 If an application doesn't offer a way to change its working folder, tell Windows to open it where you want it to save files. In Windows, right click the Start button and select Explorer, then find the shortcut to the application. Right click the shortcut, select Properties, go to the shortcut tab and type the desired working folder in the 'Start in' field.

Point the My Documents folder to any one you want

37 Even though the My Documents folder lives on your desktop, the files are actually stored in the folder found in the root of your C: drive. To change this location create a folder where you would like your documents stored (this can be called anything), then right click on the My Documents folder on your desktop and select Properties. Use the browse button to locate the new folder and select OK.

38 Explorer-less file management. You can manage files right inside your applications. The Save As and Open dialog boxes of Windows' savvy applications offer full drag-and-drop capabilities and the same right click menu you get in Explorer or a standard folder window.

39 Looking to free up some disk space? Check your Windows Help folder for AVI video files, you could have as much as 7Mb of them left over from Windows' tutorial. Unless you're using Windows for the first time, you don't need them.

Keyboard Shortcuts

40 Navigate menus using the keyboard to cut out the mouse. You can activate the current program's menu using F10, navigate around using the cursor keys and select the menu item with the Return key.

41 Quickly select buttons and menus using the Alt key. If a button or menu item has one letter underlined in its name you can select this by doing the following. Hold down the Alt key and tap the underlined letter on the keyboard. This will select the relevant item.

Quickly switch between windows using Alt+Tab

42 Switch between windows and programs running on your machine using the Tab key. By holding the Alt key and tapping the Tab key you can cycle through all the open windows. Hold the Shift key down to cycle backwards through them.

43 To close any window or program using just the keyboard press

Alt-F4. If you have no programs running this will also close windows and shutdown your computer.

44 Navigate program and window gadgets using the keyboard. The currently selected gadget or button is outlined or highlighted, use the Tab key to jump to the next button or other gadget along, select buttons by pressing return. You can jump back by holding the Shift key and pressing Tab.

45 Want to open the Start menu without using the mouse? On older keyboards press Ctrl-Esc and on new style keyboards just use the Windows key (it has the Windows logo on it). You can then navigate the Start menu using the cursor keys. Hit Return to launch the program you want.

46 Use the number pad on your keyboard to take control of the mouse cursor. Open the Accessibility Control Panel. Switch to the Mouse Tab and select Use Mouse Keys press the Settings button to adjust exactly how you want the keys to work.

47 Lost a file in all the clutter you have on your drives? In Windows press F3 to get the Find File utility. Enter all or part of the name of the file you want and click Find Now. Wait for a list of possible files to appear in the lower part of the window.

48 Do you find renaming icons a little bit tricky? An easier way than right-clicking on an icon to rename it is to select the icon and press the F2 key. Now tap in the new name for the icon.

49 You can use the Windows key to minimise and maximise the current open Windows (very handy if you need to get to the Desktop quickly). There are two ways; holding the Windows key and tapping D will open and close all the currently open windows, pressing Windows+M will just close all the Windows, while Windows+Shift+M will open all closed windows.

Tidy up your Desktop and close all the related Windows using Shift+Close window

50 If you ever get stuck using a program or cannot remember how to do a certain thing with Windows, don't get upset, press the F1 key. This opens up the help for that program.

51 If you have a Windows key you can run certain parts of Windows with the press of two buttons. To open the System Control Panel press the Windows+Break keys. If you want to run Windows Explorer press Windows+E. You can jump to the Windows run dialog by pressing Windows+R.

52 Do you open lots of Windows following folder paths? If so you can close all the parent windows in one go by holding down the Shift key and clicking the close windows button.

53 When using Windows, pressing the Backspace key will take you to the parent folder – the same job as pressing the up button from the Windows toolbar.

54 Here are some regularly used keyboard shortcuts that work with every Windows program. Press Ctrl+X to cut selected items. Ctrl+V will paste cut and copied items, while Ctrl+C will copy any selected items. To make a new document press Ctrl+N, Ctrl+O opens a document, Ctrl+S will save the current document and Ctrl+P prints the currently open files. To undo the last set of changes press Ctrl+Z. Look in the menus for listed keyboard shortcuts.

Hardware

55 Having trouble getting audio from your new USB speakers? You should check their output mode. Some USB speakers have switches that shift between digital and audio mode. Make sure you have your speakers set to Digital mode if you have them plugged in via your PC's USB ports.

56 To avoid problems with your display resolution, make sure Windows 98 correctly identifies the display adapter and monitor in the Device Manager (Start...Settings...Control Panel...System). If this information is not correct, Windows 98 may artificially restrict your resolution settings. It does this so as not to allow resolutions that are beyond the capabilities of an adapter or monitor.

57 Reversing slow notebook performance. Is your notebook slowing down or even shutting down when you have it connected to an electrical outlet? If so, you should check your BIOS settings. Under BIOS setup, most notebooks allow you to shut off the power saving features when the notebook is not running from the battery.

58 If you find that your modem is sometimes disconnecting unexpectedly, the trouble could be your 'call waiting' phone feature. With call waiting active, your modem may hang up when an incoming call beeps in on your phone line. Make sure you disable call waiting by adding the appropriate codes in your Dial-Up Networking Connect To screen.

59 Get rid of the unnecessary files that are filling up your hard drive. You'll be amazed at the number of megabytes of storage that useless files consume. Search your hard drive for unneeded image files (*.BMP) and Zip files (*.ZIP) that you've already extracted and delete the ones you won't be using.

60 If you're not satisfied with the responsiveness of your joystick during game play, you may need to calibrate it. In the Windows Start menu, choose Settings...Control Panel and you'll find a joystick icon (whether or not you have one installed). Choose this icon to bring up the Game Controllers Properties.

61 You can turn down the screeching noise your modem makes. External modems usually have a speaker volume control that allows you to quickly turn down or turn off this noise. Internal modem noise can be controlled by software. In Windows Start menu, choose Settings...Control Panel. Double click the Modem icon and select Properties, then slide the Speaker Volume control to Off.

You can stop your modem squealing by turning down its speaker

62 Never touch the gold-edged connectors on computer cards. Static electricity can easily damage the components on the card and the oil on your skin can corrode the connectors. Always handle the add-in card by its green edges or by the metal bracket at the back of the card.

63 Users often forget that you can add more than one input device to a PC under Windows. If you like the feel of a traditional mouse for most work, but prefer a trackball, touch pad or joystick for other applications or games, consider installing a second pointing device.

64 A damaged or defective IDE (hard drive controller) cable can make your system appear as if something is wrong with your hard drive. If your IDE cable goes bad, your CPU can't communicate with the hard drive and won't be able to boot the operating system. Even experts are sometimes fooled by this and will recommend a hard drive replacement when all that's needed is a new £2 cable.

65

The internal cables used to connect your CD-ROM drive to your sound card are notoriously fragile. If you have accidentally damaged a cable, you won't be able to hear any audio from your PC speakers when playing an audio CD. So, check the audio cable first when experiencing audio problems.

66

Test your rescue disks. If you've purchased any crash prevention/recovery software, such as Symantec's Norton Utilities or Helix's Nuts & Bolts, make sure that you create and then test the "rescue" disks that help you recover from system crashes. Testing the disks means booting up with the rescue disk in your A: drive to determine that your system

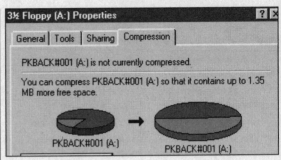

Compressing your floppy drive will let you squeeze more on it

will start successfully.

67

Trying to put off that removable storage drive purchase a little while longer? Here's a tip that might help. Windows 98's DriveSpace 3 and Compression Agent utilities (under Start...Programs...Accessories... System Tools) work on floppy disks. By compressing a floppy with these tools, you can store over 3Mb on it.

68

If you've upgraded your Notebook to Windows 98, make sure you review your power

management settings. Windows 98 supports the new ACPI (Advanced Configuration and Power Interface) standard, in addition to supporting the older APM (Advanced Power Management) power management standard. With ACPI, you can fine-tune devices to increase the life of your battery.

69

Make sure your graphics card is doing all it can. Launch the System Control Panel, then pick the Performance tab. Press the Graphics button. There you'll find the graphics hardware

Inside image:

3½ Floppy (A:) Properties

General | Tools | Sharing | Compression

PKBACK#001 (A:) is not currently compressed.

You can compress PKBACK#001 (A:) so that it contains up to 1.35 MB more free space.

PKBACK#001 (A:) → PKBACK#001 (A:)

...acceleration slider bar. Unless you have problems with your graphics accelerator, slide the bar all the way to the right.

70 When's the last time you adjusted your monitor's settings for contrast, brightness and colour balance? If you've moved your computer from one room to another it's time to do it again. A monitor's settings always relate to its environment. This means that the settings you would use for a dark room are completely different from those you would use near a window.

71 Big hard drives are cheaper than ever. For £150 to £250 you can purchase drives from 8Gb to 12Gb. Since mid range drives (3Gb or 4Gb) cost around £100, these larger drives are a real example of getting more for your money. If you're considering a new hard drive, why not load up a higher-capacity drive? You won't run out of room nearly as fast with a larger drive.

72 Hard drive upgrades, part 2: Install it as a boot drive. Large hard drives use new technologies to attain faster data transfer rates. Your best bet to take advantage of these speeds is to install the new hard drive as your boot drive, instead of adding it on as a second

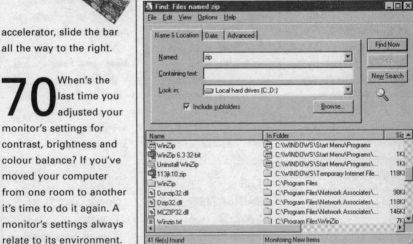

Find and remove unwanted files to save room

hard drive. Use the disk copy software included in your hard drive upgrade kit to perform this task.

73
Clean up old drives. Before you install a new hard drive and transfer your data from your old to your new drive, clean it up! Remove any temporary files, image files (BMP, GIF, TIF, etc.) and old Zip (ZIP) files that you no longer need. Review all your applications and archive or delete the ones that you don't really use. Then, make sure to defragment your drive before you start.

74
Format with FAT32. If you've upgraded to Windows 98, seriously consider formatting your new hard drive with the FAT32 file system. The biggest benefit is that you won't waste as much space with a larger disk partition as you would under the older FAT16 file

system. In fact, FAT16 doesn't support partitions larger than 2Gb, but FAT32 supports partitions greater than 32Gb.

75
CDs are rather delicate, even a single scratch can render a computer CD disc useless. So make sure you always put the discs back into their cases once you have finished with them and don't leave them lying on your desk.

Basic tips

76
Trouble resizing windows? If you find the sides of windows too thin right click a blank area of the desktop and select properties. Click the Appearance tab and

choose Active Window Border from the Item list box. Adjust the size box to a bigger number, around six is worth trying.

77
Spare parts. When you install a new board in your PC, you end up with a spare metal plate, the one used to protect the card slot's opening at the back of your PC. Where should you store this plate in case you ever need it again? Inside your PC. Tape these spare plates to the inside cover of your PC, so that he can never lose them.

78
Have you got speakers, a modem, a mike, and a phone line connected to your computer? If your answer is

Arial	**Arial**
Courier New	**Courier New**
Symbol	**Σψμβολ**
Times New Roman	**Times New Roman**

Selection of Windows fonts

yes, then you can make a phone call without even picking up the phone! Click the Start button, and choose Programs/ Accessories/ Phone Dialler. In the Number to Dial box, type the number you want to dial. Click Dial. The phone rings, you hear the person on the other end through your speakers, and you respond through the mike. To hang up, click Hang Up.

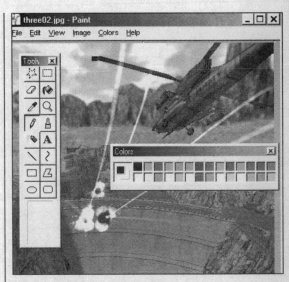

Float program palettes to provide more space

79 When you create documents in Windows, to make sure they look the same to the people you give them to restrict yourself to the standard Windows fonts which are: Arial, Courier New, Symbol, Times New Roman and Wingdings

80 Windows gives you a way to check battery power on your portable. At the right end of the taskbar, wave your mouse over the Power icon (the picture of a battery and a little plug). A small box appears, telling you Windows' estimate of how many hours of power you have remaining.

81 To float your colour palette in Paint, click above the colour palette and a box appears around the palette. Drag the box over the drawing space and release the mouse button when the box is where you want it. To return the palette to its original location, simply drag it back. You can tear away the drawing tool palette in the same way.

82 If you find icons are snapping back into place it's because you've got your desktop set to AutoArrange which keeps icons in their place. To turn it off right click on

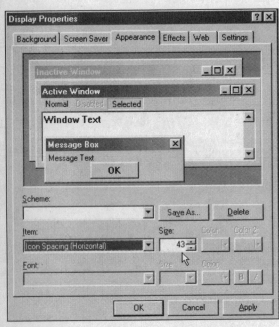

Spread out your icons by adjusting your Appearance settings

84 Add a keyboard shortcut to any program by finding it in the Start menu, right clicking on it and selecting Properties. In the window that opens select the Shortcut key text box and then press the key combination you want to run this program. Click OK when you have finished. Use this key combination to run the program whenever you want to.

85 You can reset your speaker volume without leaving any program you're in. On the right end of the Taskbar, click the yellow speaker icon. Adjust the volume by using the slider that appears. Click any blank space on the desktop to make the slider disappear. You don't have a little yellow speaker? You may have to activate it in the Multimedia Control Panel, make sure the Show Volume tick box is selected in the first Audio tab.

any blank area of the desktop, choose Arrange Icons...AutoArrange (to deselect the option). Now you can drag your icons anywhere you want.

83 Why not clone a floppy disk? Find a spare floppy disk, it doesn't have to be empty. Place the disk you want to clone in the floppy disk drive. Just click the Start button and then choose Programs...Windows Explorer. Under All Folders, find your floppy drive (usually A:), right-click it, and then choose Copy Disk from the shortcut menu and follow the instructions.

86 If you manage to lose the Windows title bar off the top of the desktop get it back by pressing Alt+Spacebar+M. Press the down arrow repeatedly until your title bar appears, you can use this technique to move a window in any direction; just press Alt+Spacebar+M and then press the appropriate arrow key.

87 I just deleted loads of files; so where's all my new free disk space? Deleting simply moves your unwanted files to the Recycle Bin, where they continue to take up the same amount of space. You're not going to get your space back until you empty the Recycle Bin, right click the Recycle Bin icon. Choose Empty Recycle Bin from the shortcut menu.

88 If you have auto arranged your icons and have since found that they are far too close together, you can get them to spread out by doing the following. Right-click any blank area of the desktop and choose Properties from the Shortcut menu.

Now click the Appearance tab and from the Item drop-down list select Icon Spacing (Horizontal), then increase the number in the Size box. In the Item drop-down list, select Icon Spacing (Vertical), then increase the number in the Size box.

89 How can I select all the text in a WordPad document? Open a document and then try any of these techniques to select all the text in that document. 1. Press Ctrl+A. Triple click in the left margin of the document. Hold down the Ctrl key and then click in the left margin. Press Ctrl+Home to move the cursor to the beginning of the document and then press Ctrl+Shift+End.

90 Got so many icons that you can scarcely see your desktop wallpaper? Free up a little desktop space by making

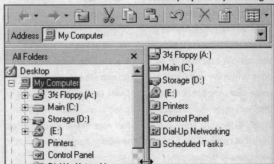

Adjust the panes in Windows Explorer to suit your needs

your icons smaller? Right click any blank area of your desktop, choose Properties from the Shortcut menu. Click the Appearance tab and, under Item, select Icons. Set the Size smaller but don't make the size too small; below 24 looked bad on our screens.

91 Noticed how Window Explorer is split into two sections (called panes)? You can resize these by clicking on the vertical bar dividing them and dragging sideways.

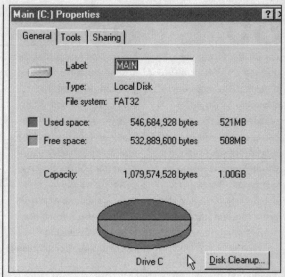

You can find out how much room is left on your drives by selecting their properties

92 If you spot a nice background pattern while surfing the Web, and if your browser is Microsoft Windows Explorer, you can set that texture as your Windows wallpaper. Right click any blank area of the Web page and choose Set as Wallpaper from the Shortcut menu. That's it. The background is now your wallpaper.

93 If you use Dos programs you may be glad you hear that you can make the Dos program fill the whole screen. To switch from a Dos window to full-screen Dos, press Alt+Enter. Even better, this switch is a toggle. So, to switch from full-screen Dos back to Dos window again, press Alt+Enter.

94 To adjust the speed Windows repeats key presses, click the Start button and choose Settings...Control Panel and double click the Keyboard icon. If necessary, click the Speed tab. Under Character Repeat, slide the slider button toward Fast. If you make the repeat rate much faster, we recommend you slide the Repeat Delay slider button toward Long.

95 Access your desktop files through a window. Double click the My Computer icon. In the toolbar's drop-down list, click Desktop. Size the window and arrange the icons any way you like by choosing View and selecting the desired options. From now on, whenever you want to get to the desktop, just click the new Desktop button on your Taskbar.

96 If you find that your mouse control seems to be getting worse and you have trouble clicking on icons, flip the mouse open and spin the panel you find till it come off. Remove the ball and clean all the dirt off the runners inside. Replace everything and you find that your mouse will run a good deal smoother than before.

97 Maximise the number of files you can see in each window by selecting View...List from the Windows menu. This uses the smallest possible icon and so you can see many more files and folders. 98It is possible to change the icons used by shortcuts. Right click on the shortcut and select Properties. In the Window that appears click the Change Icon... button and a selection of alternate icons will appear. Select one you like and click OK twice. -

99 Double click the My Computer icon to show all the drives attached to your computer then right click on a drive and select Properties and a nice pie chart will appear showing you how much space you have left.

100 If you need to use a character you cannot seem to find on the keyboard use the Character Map program. Go Start menu... Accessories...System Tools...Character Map, choose the character you want click the Select button and then copy and paste the character into your document.

Absolute Beginners:
crash course

New to Windows? We get you up to speed with the world's most popular PC software

If you're new to computers, switching your PC on for the first can be scary. All those alien screens and odd little icons can put you off computers for life!

But don't be disheartened. Over the next few pages, we're going to introduce Windows 98, the world's most popular computer operating system that comes as standard on new PCs. Windows 98, and its predecessor 95, are very easy to learn.

You perform tasks on your computer, such as writing a letter, by opening programs, or 'applications.' These applications are stored on a disk inside your computer called the 'hard disk.'

You open and close these programs and get around generally by pointing at icons with your mouse and clicking them, or by using it to pull down lists of commands or 'menus.'

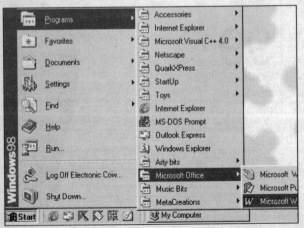

Start Menu

1 The best place to begin exploring Windows is the Start button. Click it, and a pop-up menu appears. Move to Programs, and a sub-menu will pop-out, with a list of major programs. Click on one to start it.

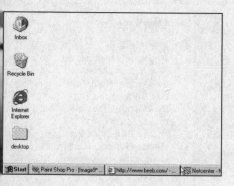

Toolbar

2 Another key feature is the toolbar, at the bottom of the screen. Every time a window is opened, or program started, an extra button is added. Click the button to bring the window to the front of any others you may have open.

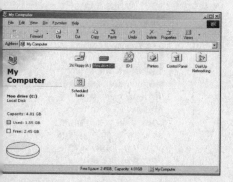

My Computer

3 Click My Computer to see icons for your hard, floppy disk and CD-ROM drives. You can click the hard drive icon (usually 'C') to see what programs are on there. Use the same method for your floppy disks and CD-ROMs.

Icons

4 Icons can be viewed big, small or as a text list (this includes details of the file's characteristics, such as its size and the date it was created). To change how icons appear in a window, click on the View menu explore the options.

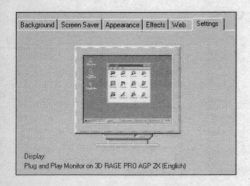

Display:
Plug and Play Monitor on 3D RAGE PRO AGP 2X (English)

Display

5 Windows' appearance can be further altered via the Display Properties box. Click on the Desktop with the right mouse button and choose Properties from the menu. Here, you can change the appearance of your desktop

Copying

6 To copy files between windows, select the files and drag the file icon from one window to another. Copy files onto floppy disks by dragging files onto the floppy icon (found under 'My Computer').

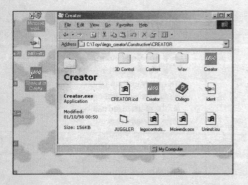

Shortcut

7 If there's a program that you use a lot, it makes sense to store its icon on your PC's Desktop so you can easily find it (make a shortcut). Select the program icon, drag it from its window and drop it on the Desktop.

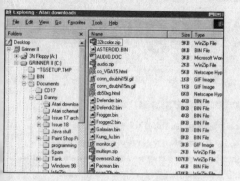

Windows Explorer

8 A quick way to find stuff is to use Windows Explorer. Go to the Start menu click the right-mouse button. A different menu will pop-up. From here choose Explore. Drives are listed on the left, files on the right.

Control Panel

9 The Control Panel lets you control how your computer (or other equipment and add-ons connected to it) behaves. To open it, click on Start, and choose Control Panels from the Settings sub-menu.

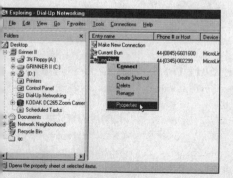

Connect

10 Once you have set up an account with an Internet service provider, you'll probably see it in a folder called Dial-Up Networking, found with My Computer or Explorer. Here, you can quickly connect and disconnect to the Net.

Absolute Beginners:
jargon busting

Computer terms explained!

Jargon can be a wonderful thing for the right people. Unfortunately, for those of us who don't understand the random jumble of letters that so accurately describes the computer world, they serve only to compound our confusion. Although we can promise that our magazine is jargon free, we unfortunately cannot make promises for everyone else. What we can do is give you a helping hand by having a crack at explaining the lingo ourselves.

Hardware A-Z

On these pages we guide you through the A-Z of Hardware, the System, Windows and Software.

Accelerator card

A card that could be fitted to a computer to make it perform faster (for instance, a graphics card fitted with VRAM instead of DRAM).

Access time

The time it takes for a device to access data. The access time, quoted in milliseconds (ms) for hard disks and nanoseconds (ns) for memory, is usually an average as it can vary greatly. Together with the transfer, it is used to gauge the performance of hard disks and other devices. The lower the number the better the performance.

Active partition

The primary partition that is set up to be read and used by the computer to boot up. The file system is read, and this becomes your 'boot up' partition.

Add-on

Hardware added to a computer after purchase to enhance ability.

Backbone site

(or server)

Web site or server that processes and directs traffic on internet/network. In a sense it performs a similar function as a CPU in an individual computer.

Bandwidth

A Network/Internet phrase which refers to how much information can be moved across the network at any one time. It refers to volume rather than speed.

Baud

Way of measuring modem speed (9600 baud rate, for example).

Bios

Internal computer chip that helps the computer think and remember what devices to use, how to communicate to the monitor and keyboard, what day it is and so forth.

Bootable

A hard drive (or floppy disk) that has the special system files on it that allows a computer to start an operating system from that disk.

Bridge

A means of connecting communications networks at different sites.

Buffer

A holding area (memory)

that stores information, keystrokes, commands, print pages and so on until the processor or device is ready for it.

Bus

In general terms, a channel along which signals travel from one of several destinations.

C Moss (CMOS)

Special battery in a computer that stores the Bios information.

Cache (disk)

There is also disk cache that is more software related, it basically hold information in memory as it is writing to the disk, and allows the user to continue without waiting until the writing is done.

Cat (i.e. Cat 5 wire)

Wire term, just short for category, thickness, how it's made and so forth.

CD-ROM

Compact Disc Read-Only Memory. These can store

up to 635Mb of data, music, sound and information. They are read by laser and cannot be copied without special hardware.

CD Writer

Hardware that will put information/files on to a CD-ROM disk.

Chips

Little 'blocks' of silicon with embedded transistor material that process information.

Client

The PC, or Workstation that is being used. The client gets information from a 'Server', but does the bulk of the processing.

Clusters

The little 'areas' on a hard drive (organised with sectors and blocks) that store files.

Computer

A machine that can be programmed to manipulate

symbols. Computers can perform complex and repetitive procedures efficiently, precisely and reliably and can quickly store and retrieve large amounts of data.

CPU (Central Processing Unit)

This is the main chip in the computer. It is the CPU that controls the operation of the computer and performs all the instructions that make up a program.

Crash

Occurs when the hard Drive fails, or a program locks up

DAT

Abbreviation for Digital Audio Tape.

Data Transfer rate

This is the speed at which data bits are transferred along a transmission channel, normally measured in bits (or kilobits or megabits) per second.

Dedicated (line)

This is a phone line that is used solely for computer connections and nothing else.

Dedicated (server/ program)

Computer/program used for only one individual task (graphic design, Web server and so forth).

Device

Just means a piece of equipment. Can be anything from a printer to a mouse, sound card to a monitor.

Digitiser

Piece of equipment that converts signals or objects into digital files or signals that a computer can read and work with.

DIMM

DIMM actually stands for Dual Inline Memory Module. An industry standard for Pentium and Pentium II memory. DIMMs are small circuit boards with RAM chips on them that mount at right angles to the motherboard.

DPI (Dots Per Inch)

Common measure of the resolution on a printer, a scanner or a display.

DRAM (Dynamic Random Access Memory)

Standard type of memory chip used in older PCs. Less efficient than SDRAM, VRAM or EDO RAM.

EDO (Extended Data Out)

A type of memory.

EISA

EISA is an abbreviation for Extended Industry Standard Architecture.

EPROM

Erasable Programmable read-only Memory. A chip that can be read from but cannot be written to, except by means of special hardware (called EPROM burners) or, with 'flash' EPROMs by means of special software.

Expanded Memory

A part of the computer's memory for special use of software and add-on boards to use memory over 640 Kb. Used in earlier years, and in some older programs.

Extended Memory

Memory above the 1st Meg or RAM – addressed by memory managers (himem.sys). Allows programs to make use of memory beyond the 640kb range.

Fax

A fax (short for facsimile) is a document transferred electronically across a telephone line. A fax machine takes a document, breaks it down into a series of dots and sends these down a telephone line where a fax machine at the other end re-constitutes them into a copy of the original document. Modems can be used to send and receive faxes.

Fibre optic

Type of 'wire' made of glass; transfers data more quickly than copper.

File server

A program running on a network that stores files and provide access to them. Also called server.

Firmware

Software instruction imbedded into 'chips' or hardware. (Can only be changed or programmed with special equipment.)

Floppy disk drive

Most PCs come with a floppy disk drive. 3.5in HD (high density) 1.44Mb floppy disks are now the standard. They come in hard plastic cases and have replaced the older, literally floppy, 5.25in disks. A slot in the front of the computer, the floppy drive is often called the 'A' drive.

Graphics card

An expansion card that interprets commands from the processor to the monitor. If you want a better, higher-resolution picture or more than your existing setup, you'll need to change your graphics card and/ or your monitor.

Hard coded

Chips or memory that contain software type instructions, programmed into them when they are created, often referred to as ROM

Hard disk

Where data's stored (often known as the 'C' drive), including system info. The size of the hard disk is measured in MB.

computer) as it is being built, as opposed to cards that can be plugged in and out after production.

Heads

Part of computer's drive that scans and reads files from disk.

Host

The computer that is sharing its resources. (Can also refer to individual PC on the Internet or a network)

Hub

A Hub is a device that connects together all computers in a star-type formation network.

I/O

Input Output (type a letter = input, print the letter = output), but can also refer to more complex instructions that the computer uses internally to process information and where in memory the process is to occur.

Hard wired

Refers to chips, ports, or devices connected to motherboard (or

Inkjet

Printer type where ink is sprayed on to the paper through tiny holes or jets.

Interlaced

Refers to how a monitor displays information. Interlaced means the projection is shown in rows of pixels (dots of light), each row is redrawn separately. This makes for lower quality than non-interlaced which refreshes each pixel independently.

ISA

Industry Standard Architecture. This was the original bus architecture on 286 PCs. Also known as the AT bus (the 286 was known as the AT), it is still in use today. Slow by modern standards, but so widely accepted that expansion cards are still made for it.

Jaz drive

Special type of drive and disk that can be hooked to a computer. Holds either 1Gb or 2Gb on data and programs. (Fairly similar to Zip drives.)

Jumper

A physical switch used to change the settings of a device. A jumper consists of two parts; a bank of two or more pins and a cap – a metal lined plastic cover that covers two pins. When a jumper cap is in place there is an electrical connection between the two pins. In this state the jumper is said to be closed (and with the cap off, it said to be open).

Keyboard

A device used to enter text into a computer system or terminal.

LAN (Local Area Network)

A computer network technology that connects computers separated by a short distance.

Laptop

Small computer that is portable and will run on batteries.

Laser Printer

Laser printers work by heat transfer – much the same as photocopiers. Information is transferred from your PC to the laser printer and all print is heat transferred to give a high quality print on paper.

LED (Light Emitting Diode)

A device that lights up when electricity flows through it in a given direction. As it is a diode it stops electricity flowing though it in the opposite direction.

Lost clusters

Areas of a hard drive which once contained files.Even though the files have been moved or deleted, the information was not reported to the computers file system that this area of the disk is now free.

Master

Usually refers to the primary disk/drive that a computer boots from.

Maths co-processor

A special chip that performs mathematical calculations (floating point operations) for the processor. Most modern processors such as the Pentium have co-processors built in as standard.

Media

Type of disk, or tape that information is stored on (ie. CD, Tape, Floppy)

Microprocessor

A very small processor (created with silicon and transistor material) capable of directing, calculating and processing large amounts of information very quickly.

Modem

Device used to send information from one computer to another using a telephone.

Monitor

Your computers' screen. Signals are sent to it from the video card.

Mouse
The little hand-size device with button(s) used to control computer functions.

Network
Hardware and software data communication systems

Networked
Group of computers hooked together that can share information and programs

Node
A general term meaning a point in a communications network at which several transmission lines meet.

Notebook
Small 'laptop' computer, named for its size.

Parallel Port
A parallel port is most typically used for printers as a form of communication transfer.

Mother Board
The "Main" board inside a computer case that connects all the other components.

Partition
A portion of a hard drive which has been sectioned off to represent a specific drive eg: C:, D:, E: drives could all be separate partitions of the same hard disc.

PCI (Peripheral Component Interconnect)
Developed by Intel, it is now the standard for local bus architecture. Faster than VL-Bus (Video Electronic Standards Association local bus) it replaces.

PCMCIA
A standard to allow PC, particularly notebooks, to be expanded using credit-card size cards.

Pentium
Pentium processors are Intel's current range of PC processors. Processors used to be identified by number (286, 386, 486), instead of moving to 586 from 486, Intel changed

the processor's name to Pentium. The Pentium processor has had a number of revisions since its release, bringing about the Pentium II, Pentium MMX, and Pentium III.

Peripheral

Piece of equipment attached to a computer

Plug-in

One of a set of software modules that integrate into Web browsers to offer a wide range of interactive and multimedia capabilities.

Primary Partition

The part of the Hard Disk that is used to start the computer. (Can be more than 1 - but only one primary boot partition can be active at a given time)

Processor

Part of the computer: brain that directs and processes information, often called the CPU in IBM clone computers.

RAM (Random Access Memory)

The term normally given to memory. This is the kind that disappears when you turn off your computer and is much faster to access than a hard disk. It acts as a staging post between your computer's hard disk and its main processor.

Refresh rate

Refers to how often (or fast) a monitor redraws the image on the screen.

ROM

Read Only Memory. These chips hold data that can be read but not written to, can be used to run checks on a computer and then load up the operating system.

Router

Network hardware: creates connection between 2 of the same types of networks

Scanner

Convert paper based information into a style that can be held on a computer.

SCSI (Small Computer Systems Interface)

Small Computer Systems Interface is a bus that comes as standard in Macintosh and is starting to rival EIDE on PCs.

Serial Port

A place where you connect all the extras required to access the computer e.g. mouse, modem etc.

Server

A computer that offers services on a network.

SIMM (Single Inline Memory Module)

The Single Inline Memory Module is the standard module for memory expansion on PCs. Older 30-pin SIMMs have now been replaced by the 72-pin variety available in capacities of up to 16Mb.

Slave

Slave usually refers to a second disk/drive in a computer where one drive is designated as the master.

Spooler

A holding area for printing that organises what gets printed when, and how fast it gets sent.

SRAM

Static Random Access Memory. It is called "static" because it will retain a value as long as power is supplied, unlike dynamic random access memory (DRAM), which must be regularly refreshed. It is however, still volatile, i.e. it will lose its contents when the power is switched off, in contrast to ROM. SRAM is usually faster than DRAM, and it usually costs more than DRAM and so is used for the most speed-critical parts of a computer.

Stand Alone

A computer not hooked up to a network

Switches

Special Internet or network computers, or hardware that direct traffic and route information to the proper address.

Tape Streamer

Magnetic tape recorder for backing up data from a hard disk.

Terminator

A device that 'caps off' a network line, informing the signal that it is travelling on the line of the end of the network and that it should return back to the beginning.

Topology

Layout of all computers, equipment, cables, and links on network.

Trackball

Pointing device with large ball (usually manipulated by thumb) used to move mouse arrow around.

UPS (Un-interruptible Power Supply)

A device that will allow a PC to continue running for a short period of time in the event of a power cut.

USB (Universal Serial Bus)

A new standard for allowing multiple serial devices (modems, mice, keyboards etc.) to be daisy chained. There are currently very few peripherals that support USB.

WAN (Wide Area Network)

A computer network that spans a long distance and that uses specialised computers to connect smaller networks.

Worm

A Type of CD Writer (can 'Write Once, and Read Many).

Write Protect

Making a file (or entire disk) so that it can be read, but not changed. This can be done with tabs and stickers on floppy disk.

Zip Drive

Type of storage disk and drive that connects to a computer. Holds 100 Mb per disk.

System A-Z

And here is our guide through the A-Z of your system.

ASCII

American Standard Code of Information Interchange. It uses 7 bits to represent all uppercase and lowercase characters, as well as numbers, punctuation marks, and other characters. ASCII often uses 8 bits in the form of bytes and ignores the first bit.

Backdoor

A hidden or undocumented login account or access level to a program or system - often left by programmers so they can get back in to a system at an administrative level in case of an emergency, or system lock-up.

Binary

Base two. A number representation consisting of 0's and 1's used by practically all computers because of its ease of implementation using digital electronics and Boolean algebra.

Bit

Short for Binary digiT. a piece of information, so you hear about 8,16 or 32 bit chunks of data. The bigger the number the more can be handled in one go.

Byte

A single character or instruction of computer language

Cache (Memory)

Special area of memory that stores recent commands so they can be executed faster than calling the information back from the Hard Drive again

Clone

A Clone is actually a computer that is 100% compatible with the IBM/Intel standards.

Code

verb: To write a program
noun: The instructions a program carries out

DMA (Direct Memory Access)

A function of certain expansion bus architectures that allows a device to directly access a computer's memory.

DOS (Disk Operating System)

The operating system of the computer. DOS is a basic text based operating system unlike Windows

which is a graphical operating system. DOS was the original PC operating system, and over the years there have been several versions of it. The most common DOS on PCs is MS-DOS from Microsoft who wrote the original version of DOS for the PC. There have been other versions of DOS from other software vendors such as Novell. Other versions of DOS include PC-DOS and DR-DOS, neither of which is commonly used any more. Windows type operating systems are rapidly replacing DOS, although they all include a facility to run DOS applications.

DOS Prompt

You'll see a DOS Prompt when you exit Windows – it is the place where you type on the screen " C:\> "

Drivers

Files that contain instruction on how to communicate with other hardware/software.

End User

Person who will ultimately use a program (or hardware) to organise data. The end user of a word processor is the person who actually types up a letter, and prints it.

Error

Any instance where the expected results are not achieved.

FAQ (Frequently Asked Questions)

A common type of document on the Internet that contains a list of questions and answers on a common theme. On the World Wide Web, questions are often hyperlinks to the answers.

Fatal Error

A Fatal Error is an error that has confused your processor so much that it needs to be restarted.

FAT

File Allocation Table: special information stored on a PC's hard drive that tells it where the files are stored, and what their names are. (FAT32 is the new design for the Windows 98 file system.)

Flow Chart

Schematic diagram of how a program will work.

Fonts

A font is an alphabet designed in a particular Style. Fonts apply to both screen and printed letters. True Type and Type1 fonts are stored as shape descriptions, scaleable to any size.

Gigabyte (Gb)

A gigabyte is 1000 megabytes.

GUI (Graphical User Interface)

Windows is a GUI developed by Microsoft. Windows is intended to make programs easier to use by giving them a standard, mouse driven interface.

Hex

A numbering system used in computers where there are 16 possible places (base 16 format uses letters to assign values) binary=(base 2), and people use base 10.

High End

The upper end product a company offers (either hardware or software) usually geared toward business use due to complexity, features, and price

High Memory

Memory between 1st 640 Kb (conventional), and 1 Mb of RAM memory. This is usually reserved for video drivers and programs.

Image

To copy a disk by byte and sector, rather than just the files.

Initialise

To start up, when referring to disks it means to format them so they can be used.

Interrupt

Setting the computer looks for that manages "who" the processor talks to. ex. If you press the escape key, printing stops. The keyboard 'interrupted the print processing.

IRQ

Interrupt ReQuest - allows devices to communicate directly with the CPU in a predefined sequence. Each hardware device that requires one is assigned an IRQ, then for a predefined length of time the CPU will access each IRQ line in turn, allowing the hardware device on that particular IRQ to talk to the CPU.

Kb

Abbreviation for Kilobyte

Kb or K

A kilobyte = 1024 bytes

Kernel

The main instruction set of the computers operating system (loaded into memory on startup)

Mb (megabyte)

A megabyte is 1000 kilobytes.

Mb or M

A Megabyte = 1,048,576 bytes

Memory Manager(s)

Software programs that address memory over conventional 640 Kb.

Network

Hardware and software data communication systems

Octal (octet)

Numbering system that uses 8 places/digits for addressing - used in IP addressing

OEM

Abbreviation for Original equipment Manufacturer.

Operating System

(OS) The low-level software which schedules tasks, allocates storage, handles the interface to peripheral hardware and presents a default interface to the user when no application program is running

Parity

A redundant way of checking information validity (usually odd, or even), by setting aside a 'bit' to 1 or 0 to validate the preceding 7 bits of information thus creating a byte. Often used in communication, and older memory checking.

Plug and Play

Refers to late 90's technology were software and hardware talk to one another so if a user adds a device, it sets its self up automatically when installed.

Snail mail

The regular 'Post Office' method of sending paper mail (see email)

Star dot Star shown (*.*)

A way of defining EVERYTHING (all characters beforehand after the "."

SVGA

Super Video Graphics Array - an enhanced version of VGA. Unlike VGA SVGA tends to be proprietary, with exact specifications varying from manufacturer to manufacturer. While a VGA display driver would work with any video card, SVGA drives are specific to a particular video card. SVGA offers higher resolutions and greater colour depths than VGA - up to resolutions of 1600 by 1200 (this is only possible with very powerful video cards though) and up to 32bit colour (16.7 million colours).

UNIX

A portable operating system, able to operate on a wide range of computer systems from mainframes down to personal computers.

VR (Virtual Reality)

Refers to how real and 3 dimensional games, and Internet technology have become.

Win.ini

The win.ini file for Windows systems. Defines users settings (colors, etc.)

Year 2000

Problem that involves how computers remember the date. If a computer only remembers the last 2 digits of the year, then when it gives that date to the operating system or program, it may think the year 2000 is actually 1900. Now been addressed in recent versions of Windows.

Windows A-Z

Active desktop

New Windows 98 technology: makes your wallpaper interactive- links can be made in the wallpaper, news / information can be displayed and updated as wallpaper.

Cascade (windows)

Method of displaying 'Windows' so that edges of each are displayed with one on top of the other (method similar to the way cards are displayed in solitaire).

Cell

Single block of information in spreadsheet programs (spreadsheets often are math oriented applications).

Check box

A form field that presents the user with a selection that can be chosen by clicking on a box. When the box is selected, it is usually displayed with a check mark or X. Check boxes can represent a set of non-exclusive choices.

Chicago

Code name for the Windows 95 program code.

Click

To push a mouse button.

Clipboard

A temporary storage area on the computer for cut or copied items.

Column

In a table, a vertical collection of cells.

Command line

An interface that utilises keyboard commands to execute commands rather than using a mouse to click on items.

Control Panel

Windows folder where settings can be configured.

Cursor

In DOS it is the blinking line or box after the C:\>, in Windows it usually refers to where the mouse pointer is, or area of program where typing will occur.

Cut and Paste

Process of removing something (picture, text, etc.) from one program or file and putting it into another. Cut differs from copy in that you remove the original when you cut and you make a duplicate when you copy.

Daemon

Program that runs in the background collecting data or doing computer administration tasks.

Defrag (to Defragment)

To clean up a disk by moving and organising all the files so all parts of the same file are all together in same place on the disk / Hard Drive.

Dialog Box

A box outline that appears on the screen with a message.

DirectX

An add-on to Windows 95

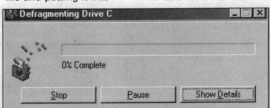

that allows programmers to communicate directly with the hardware. There have been several versions of DirectX, the latest of which is DirectX 5.

Directory (Folder)

An area on the disk where files are stored. You can have lots of them and they hold associated information.

Double-Click

To push the mouse button twice in rapid succession.

Drag (Drag & Drop)

To move something in Windows by 'clicking' on something, holding the button down, and 'Drag' (or move) it to somewhere else.

Explorer

Refers to Windows95 version of file manager and Microsoft's Internet browser.

Folder

In a URL, a single part of the path to a page. A folder is a named storage area on the computer containing files and other folders.

GPF - General Protection Fault

When a piece of software crashes it in many cases will have caused a general protection fault. There are lots or reasons why a piece of software causes a GPF. When one occurs in Windows 95 a dialog box will tell you the error has occurred. If you click on "details", Windows displays information about the fault, which can be useful for technical support.

Heading

A paragraph type that is displayed in a large, bold typeface. The size of a heading is related to its level: Heading 1 is the largest, Heading 2, the next largest, and so on. Use headings to name pages and parts of pages.

Icon

Little picture on a computer screen or window linked to a program or command.

Launch

To start a program.

Macro

Programming within an application e.g. making commands a keystroke.

Map (Map a drive)

Assigning a drive letter to another computer, drive, or directory on a network.

Memphis

Code name for the Windows 98 program code.

MPEG

Technology for viewing video (both hardware, and software).

Paste

To copy something in Windows from 1 application to another.

Point (Point and Click)

Using a mouse to move the arrow (or cursor) to desired place on computer screen.

Profile

The access, passwords, settings, etc. networks establish for users when they login.

Radio button

A form field that presents the user with a selection that can be chosen by clicking on a button. Radio buttons are presented in a list, one of which is selected by default. Selecting a new member of the list deselects the currently selected item.

Recycle Bin

Special program (with Windows 95, NT 4, or higher) that remembers files that have been deleted, so they can be recovered later.

Registry

Database of programs and settings used by Windows (versions 95 and higher store even more information here) - current settings like screen colour, icons, type of hardware used, etc.

Scandisk

Program that checks your disks for errors and fixes them.

Screen saver

Special program that runs graphical images on your monitor when the keyboard or mouse have not been

used for a certain amount of time. Help avoid an image being burned in to the monitor causing a ghost like background.

Scroll

To move around in Windows by using the mouse, and window bars and buttons.

Shortcut

New name for the Icons in Windows 95.

Swap File

Special file on hard drive that holds information that overflows from Ram/memory.

Task Bar

Windows 95 bar (with Start Button) that acts as a central control panel for the Operating System.

Thumbnail

A small version of an image on a World Wide Web page, often containing a hyperlink to a full-size version of the image.

Tray

Small area in Windows 95 where the clock and loaded program icons reside.

Tree

Graphical display of a hierarchical file system (DOS, UNIX, Windows, etc.) A good example of this is Windows Explorer.

Truetype (font)

Fonts that are seen on the screen as they would appear on printed paper.

Virtual Memory

Method of setting aside a file on a hard drive for use as memory (see swap file).

Win ini

The win.ini file for Windows systems. Defines users settings (colours, etc.).

Window

A block or frame that a program, group of icons or other information sits in. This can be moved around the screen, minimised, maximised to fill the whole screen, or sized to preference. This is the core technology behind Graphical Environments.

Windows 95(Win95)

Microsoft's successor to their Windows 3.11 operating system for IBM PCs. It was known as "Chicago" during development. Its release was originally scheduled for late 1994 but eventually happened on 24 Aug 1995.

Windows NT

(Windows New Technology, NT). Microsoft's 32-bit operating system developed from what was originally intended to be OS/2 3.0 before Microsoft and IBM ceased joint development of OS/2. NT was designed for high end workstations (Windows NT 3.1), servers (Windows NT 3.1 Advanced Server) and corporate networks.

Windows

Operating system that uses a graphical interface (mouse point and click) instead of typed commands as in DOS.

Word Processor

Computer program used mainly to type documents, letters, memos, etc. It often has additional capabilities such as spell checking, graphics, etc

Software A-Z

ActiveX

Technology that improves video and audio output.

Applications

An application, or package, is one or more programs used for a particular task. For example: word processing, invoicing or spreadsheeting.

Archive

To remove old files either by storing them on other disks, tapes, or computers OR compressing them into smaller zip files.

Assembler

Very low level programming language that can directly access memory, hardware, etc.

Just one step above machine code (all 1's and 0's) that a computer understands.

Associations

Refers to how the computer sees file extensions (the 3 letters after a full stop) and if that extension is registered to a specific program. (bmp extension may be registered to Windows Paint)

Attributes

Special settings that can apply to files or directories that say they can be hidden, or marked as read only etc.

Autoexec (dot bat)

Special file used to execute commands when the computer starts up

Backup

A copy of important files put in a safe place that can be reloaded in the case of a crash or virus.

Backward compatible

New systems designed to accept older hardware and software

Batch (Batch File)

Multiple commands or procedures run at one time. A batch file is a special DOS file that will execute multiple commands by running 1 file.

Beta

Program or system that has been written and is in the process of being tested and fine-tuned, but not ready for sale yet.

Boot (Re-Boot)

To start up a computer (or restart)

Boot Disk

Normally a floppy disk that has a special configuration (i.e. to run a game that

needs a lot of memory) that is put into the computer so that it starts with an alternative configuration.

Bootleg

Computer software that has been stolen or copied illegally

Bug

Program code that causes a computer to malfunction or doesn't work as intended

Clip art

A collection of icons, buttons, and other generally useful graphics files that can be inserted into pages.

Cold Boot

Start a computer by turning the power off and then turning it on.

COMMAND. COM

The command line interpreter. A key system file that interprets the commands typed at the DOS prompt.

Compile

To convert written instructions (code) into programs for computers to understand.

CONFIG.SYS

One of the key system files in DOS and Windows 95. The config.sys contains the instructions to load some key device drivers.

Control Alt Delete

3 keys often pressed at the same time to shut down programs or restart a computer (Ctrl+Alt+Del)

Corrupted (files / download)

Means the entire file is not intact or proper order because something has written over part of it, or a program has changed it in some way that it is not readable.

Database

Computer program used to store information in "Records" and "Fields" containing information. (eg. Names and phone numbers; items and serial numbers; etc.)

Debug

To test / re-write a program; remove problems, and cleaning unnecessary code

Desktop Publishing

Creating graphic publications (artwork, text, graphs, tables, etc.) with a computer and software.

Device Driver

A piece of software that controls how a piece of hardware works.

Emulator

Program that "pretends" or "acts as" another program, operating system, or platform.

Fdisk

Special program used to set up 'partitions' on a hard drive.

A named collection of information that is stored on a computer disk.

File type

The format of a file (text file, picture etc.), usually indicated by its filename extension.

Freeware

Freeware is software which you can actually download from the Internet and best of all – it is free.

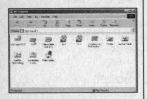

Gooey (GUI)

Graphical User Interface as opposed to the command line seen in MS-DOS. Type of interaction where a mouse is used to point and click on 'buttons' or menu items to execute instructions to computer.

Initialise

To start up, when referring to disks it means to format them so they can be used.

Interface

Just means basically 2 devices communicating with each other. Can refer to the type of system being used to interact with the computer (keyboard, mouse, scanner, etc.)

Loop

Section of code that repeats over and over often checking for a particular condition.

Macro

Macro is the term given to programming within an application e.g. making commands a keystroke.

Multimedia

Integration of sounds, pictures, animation and text together.

Multi-Tasking

Being able to do 2 things at one time eg: printing a letter with your word processor whilst are adding names to your database program, or playing a computer game.

OCR

Optical Character Recognition. Converts scanned images into text files.

OLE

Object Linking and Embedding. You can edit the image or file you have imported by double-clicking and you will return to original application.

Operating System(OS)

The low-level software which schedules tasks, allocates storage, handles the interface to peripheral hardware and presents a default interface to the user when no application program is running

Optimise

To remove or clean files and adjust settings (configurations) so that the PC runs as fast and error free, as hardware will permit.

PK Zip

Special software that can compress large files into a small file

Properties

Properties are actually the settings and values that characterise an item such as the file name and path of a file.

Query

A request for a particular item of information from a data file or a database.

Rendering

Creation of a 3-D image by creating a skeleton (called wire frame), then covering it with colour and texture.

Row

In a table, a horizontal collection of cells.

RTF (Rich Text Format)

A method of encoding text formatting and document structure using the ASCII character set. By convention, RTF files have an .RTF filename extension.

Script

Computer code that can be directly executed by a program that understands the language in which the script is written. Scripts don't need to be compiled into object code to be executed.

Shareware

Programs you can download from the Internet that request you send money if you use more than a particular time. Often smaller, limited use programs.

Shrink ware

Software purchased over the shelf through the store.

Spreadsheet

Computer program setup like graph paper. Information is put into each 'block' (called a cell). Program is good at doing calculations.

Table

A row of cells on a page used to organise the layout of a page or arrange data. In FrontPage, you can place anything in a table cell, including text, images, forms, and WebBot components.

Thumbnail

A small version of an image on a Web page, often containing a link to a full-sized version of the image.

TSR - Terminate Stay Resident

A program which when loaded stays in memory and remains active but returns control of the computer back to the user.

Vector

Graphic image file that uses lines and mathematical equations to form the picture.

VGA (Video Graphics Adapter)

A name given to a popular display. VGA has 640 pixels horizontally and 480 vertically, and can display 16 colours.

Virus

Computer instructions (code) that attaches itself to a program with the intent to cause harm - can range from annoying to destroying information.

Warm Boot

Restart a PC by pressing the Ctrl, Alt, and Delete keys (not turning off the power.)

White Space

Area on a printed page (or screen) that do not contain text or graphics.

Word Processor

Program used mainly to type documents, letters, memos, etc. Often have additional capabilities: spell checking, graphics, etc.

WYSIWYG

(What You See Is What You Get). An editing interface where the file being created is displayed as it will appear to the end-user.